THEOLOGICO-POLITICAL TREATISE — PART 1
BY
Benedictus de Spinoza

THEOLOGICO-POLITICAL TREATISE — PART 1

Published by Dossier Press

New York City, NY

First published circa 1677

Copyright © Dossier Press, 2015

All rights reserved

ABOUT DOSSIER PRESS

Since the moment people have been writing, they've been writing non-fiction works, from the *Histories* of Herodotus to the Code of Hammurabi. **Dossier Press** publishes all of the classic non-fiction works ever written and makes them available to new and old readers alike at the touch of a button.

PREFACE.

(1)Men would never be superstitious, if they could govern all their circumstances by set rules, or if they were always favoured by fortune: but being frequently driven into straits where rules are useless, and being often kept fluctuating pitiably between hope and fear by the uncertainty of fortune's greedily coveted favours, they are consequently, for the most part, very prone to credulity. (2) The human mind is readily swayed this way or that in times of doubt, especially when hope and fear are struggling for the mastery, though usually it is boastful, over - confident, and vain.

(3) This as a general fact I suppose everyone knows, though few, I believe, know their own nature; no one can have lived in the world without observing that most people, when in prosperity, are so over-brimming with wisdom (however inexperienced they may be), that they take every offer of advice as a personal insult, whereas in adversity they know not where to turn, but beg and pray for counsel from every passer-by. (4) No plan is then too futile, too absurd, or too fatuous for their adoption; the most frivolous causes will raise them to hope, or plunge them into despair - if anything happens during their fright which reminds them of some past good or ill, they think it portends a happy or unhappy issue, and therefore (though it may have proved abortive a hundred times before) style it a lucky or unlucky omen. (5) Anything which excites their astonishment they believe to be a portent signifying the anger of the gods or of the Supreme Being, and, mistaking superstition for religion, account it impious not to avert the evil with prayer and sacrifice. (6) Signs and wonders of this sort they conjure up perpetually, till one might think Nature as mad as themselves, they interpret her so fantastically.

(7) Thus it is brought prominently before us, that superstition's chief victims are those persons who greedily covet temporal advantages; they it is, who (especially when they are in danger, and cannot help themselves) are wont with Prayers and womanish tears to implore help from God: upbraiding Reason as blind, because she cannot show a sure path to the shadows they pursue, and rejecting human wisdom as vain; but believing the phantoms of imagination, dreams, and other childish absurdities, to be the very oracles of Heaven. (8) As though God had turned away from the wise, and written His decrees, not in the mind of man but in the entrails of beasts, or left them to be proclaimed by the inspiration and instinct of fools, madmen, and birds. Such is the unreason to which terror can drive mankind!

(9) Superstition, then, is engendered, preserved, and fostered by fear. If anyone desire an example, let him take Alexander, who only began superstitiously to seek guidance from seers, when he first learnt to fear fortune in the passes of Sysis (Curtius, v. 4); whereas after he had conquered Darius he consulted prophets no more, till a second time frightened by reverses. (10) When the Scythians were provoking a battle, the Bactrians had deserted, and he himself was lying sick of his wounds, "he once more turned to superstition, the mockery of human wisdom, and bade Aristander, to whom he confided his credulity, inquire the issue of affairs with sacrificed victims." (11) Very numerous examples of a like nature might be cited, clearly showing the fact, that only while under the dominion of fear do men fall a prey to superstition;

that all the portents ever invested with the reverence of misguided religion are mere phantoms of dejected and fearful minds; and lastly, that prophets have most power among the people, and are most formidable to rulers, precisely at those times when the state is in most peril. (12) I think this is sufficiently plain to all, and will therefore say no more on the subject.

(13) The origin of superstition above given affords us a clear reason for the fact, that it comes to all men naturally, though some refer its rise to a dim notion of God, universal to mankind, and also tends to show, that it is no less inconsistent and variable than other mental hallucinations and emotional impulses, and further that it can only be maintained by hope, hatred, anger, and deceit; since it springs, not from reason, but solely from the more powerful phases of emotion. (14) Furthermore, we may readily understand how difficult it is, to maintain in the same course men prone to every form of credulity. (15) For, as the mass of mankind remains always at about the same pitch of misery, it never assents long to any one remedy, but is always best pleased by a novelty which has not yet proved illusive.

(16) This element of inconsistency has been the cause of many terrible wars and revolutions; for, as Curtius well says (lib. iv. chap. 10): "The mob has no ruler more potent than superstition," and is easily led, on the plea of religion, at one moment to adore its kings as gods, and anon to execrate and abjure them as humanity's common bane. (17) Immense pains have therefore been taken to counteract this evil by investing religion, whether true or false, with such pomp and ceremony, that it may rise superior to every shock, and be always observed with studious reverence by the whole people—a system which has been brought to great perfection by the Turks, for they consider even controversy impious, and so clog men's minds with dogmatic formulas, that they leave no room for sound reason, not even enough to doubt with.

(18) But if, in despotic statecraft, the supreme and essential mystery be to hoodwink the subjects, and to mask the fear, which keeps them down, with the specious garb of religion, so that men may fight as bravely for slavery as for safety, and count it not shame but highest honour to risk their blood and their lives for the vainglory of a tyrant; yet in a free state no more mischievous expedient could be planned or attempted. (19) Wholly repugnant to the general freedom are such devices as enthralling men's minds with prejudices, forcing their judgment, or employing any of the weapons of quasi-religious sedition; indeed, such seditions only spring up, when law enters the domain of speculative thought, and opinions are put on trial and condemned on the same footing as crimes, while those who defend and follow them are sacrificed, not to public safety, but to their opponents' hatred and cruelty. (20) If deeds only could be made the grounds of criminal charges, and words were always allowed to pass free, such seditions would be divested of every semblance of justification, and would be separated from mere controversies by a hard and fast line.

(20) Now, seeing that we have the rare happiness of living in a republic, where everyone's judgment is free and unshackled, where each may worship God as his conscience dictates, and where freedom is esteemed before all things dear and precious, I have believed that I should be undertaking no ungrateful or unprofitable task, in demonstrating that not only can such freedom be granted without prejudice to the public peace, but also, that without such freedom, piety

cannot flourish nor the public peace be secure.

(21) Such is the chief conclusion I seek to establish in this treatise; but, in order to reach it, I must first point out the misconceptions which, like scars of our former bondage, still disfigure our notion of religion, and must expose the false views about the civil authority which many have most impudently advocated, endeavouring to turn the mind of the people, still prone to heathen superstition, away from its legitimate rulers, and so bring us again into slavery. (22) As to the order of my treatise I will speak presently, but first I will recount the causes which led me to write.

(23) I have often wondered, that persons who make a boast of professing the Christian religion, namely, love, joy, peace, temperance, and charity to all men, should quarrel with such rancorous animosity, and display daily towards one another such bitter hatred, that this, rather than the virtues they claim, is the readiest criterion of their faith. (24) Matters have long since come to such a pass, that one can only pronounce a man Christian, Turk, Jew, or Heathen, by his general appearance and attire, by his frequenting this or that place of worship, or employing the phraseology of a particular sect - as for manner of life, it is in all cases the same. (25) Inquiry into the cause of this anomaly leads me unhesitatingly to ascribe it to the fact, that the ministries of the Church are regarded by the masses merely as dignities, her offices as posts of emolument - in short, popular religion may be summed up as respect for ecclesiastics. (26) The spread of this misconception inflamed every worthless fellow with an intense desire to enter holy orders, and thus the love of diffusing God's religion degenerated into sordid avarice and ambition. (27) Every church became a theatre, where orators, instead of church teachers, harangued, caring not to instruct the people, but striving to attract admiration, to bring opponents to public scorn, and to preach only novelties and paradoxes, such as would tickle the ears of their congregation. (28) This state of things necessarily stirred up an amount of controversy, envy, and hatred, which no lapse of time could appease; so that we can scarcely wonder that of the old religion nothing survives but its outward forms (even these, in the mouth of the multitude, seem rather adulation than adoration of the Deity), and that faith has become a mere compound of credulity and prejudices - aye, prejudices too, which degrade man from rational being to beast, which completely stifle the power of judgment between true and false, which seem, in fact, carefully fostered for the purpose of extinguishing the last spark of reason! (29) Piety, great God! and religion are become a tissue of ridiculous mysteries; men, who flatly despise reason, who reject and turn away from understanding as naturally corrupt, these, I say, these of all men, are thought, 0 lie most horrible! to possess light from on High. (30) Verily, if they had but one spark of light from on High, they would not insolently rave, but would learn to worship God more wisely, and would be as marked among their fellows for mercy as they now are for malice; if they were concerned for their opponents' souls, instead of for their own reputations, they would no longer fiercely persecute, but rather be filled with pity and compassion.

(31) Furthermore, if any Divine light were in them, it would appear from their doctrine. (32) I grant that they are never tired of professing their wonder at the profound mysteries of Holy Writ; still I cannot discover that they teach anything but speculations of Platonists and Aristotelians, to

which (in order to save their credit for Christianity) they have made Holy Writ conform; not content to rave with the Greeks themselves, they want to make the prophets rave also; showing conclusively, that never even in sleep have they caught a glimpse of Scripture's Divine nature. (33) The very vehemence of their admiration for the mysteries plainly attests, that their belief in the Bible is a formal assent rather than a living faith: and the fact is made still more apparent by their laying down beforehand, as a foundation for the study and true interpretation of Scripture, the principle that it is in every passage true and divine. (34) Such a doctrine should be reached only after strict scrutiny and thorough comprehension of the Sacred Books (which would teach it much better, for they stand in need no human factions), and not be set up on the threshold, as it were, of inquiry.

(35) As I pondered over the facts that the light of reason is not only despised, but by many even execrated as a source of impiety, that human commentaries are accepted as divine records, and that credulity is extolled as faith; as I marked the fierce controversies of philosophers raging in Church and State, the source of bitter hatred and dissension, the ready instruments of sedition and other ills innumerable, I determined to examine the Bible afresh in a careful, impartial, and unfettered spirit, making no assumptions concerning it, and attributing to it no doctrines, which I do not find clearly therein set down. (36) With these precautions I constructed a method of Scriptural interpretation, and thus equipped proceeded to inquire - what is prophecy? (37) In what sense did God reveal himself to the prophets, and why were these particular men - chosen by him? (38) Was it on account of the sublimity of their thoughts about the Deity and nature, or was it solely on account of their piety? (39) These questions being answered, I was easily able to conclude, that the authority of the prophets has weight only in matters of morality, and that their speculative doctrines affect us little.

(40) Next I inquired, why the Hebrews were called God's chosen people, and discovering that it was only because God had chosen for them a certain strip of territory, where they might live peaceably and at ease, I learnt that the Law revealed by God to Moses was merely the law of the individual Hebrew state, therefore that it was binding on none but Hebrews, and not even on Hebrews after the downfall of their nation. (41) Further, in order to ascertain, whether it could be concluded from Scripture, that the human understanding standing is naturally corrupt, I inquired whether the Universal Religion, the Divine Law revealed through the Prophets and Apostles to the whole human race, differs from that which is taught by the light of natural reason, whether miracles can take place in violation of the laws of nature, and if so, whether they imply the existence of God more surely and clearly than events, which we understand plainly and distinctly through their immediate natural causes.

(42) Now, as in the whole course of my investigation I found nothing taught expressly by Scripture, which does not agree with our understanding, or which is repugnant thereto, and as I saw that the prophets taught nothing, which is not very simple and easily to be grasped by all, and further, that they clothed their teaching in the style, and confirmed it with the reasons, which would most deeply move the mind of the masses to devotion towards God, I became thoroughly convinced, that the Bible leaves reason absolutely free, that it has nothing in common with

philosophy, in fact, that Revelation and Philosophy stand on different footings. In order to set this forth categorically and exhaust the whole question, I point out the way in which the Bible should be interpreted, and show that all of spiritual questions should be sought from it alone, and not from the objects of ordinary knowledge. (43) Thence I pass on to indicate the false notions, which have from the fact that the multitude - ever prone to superstition, and caring more for the shreds of antiquity for eternal truths - pays homage to the Books of the Bible, rather than to the Word of God. (44) I show that the Word of God has not been revealed as a certain number of books, was displayed to the prophets as a simple idea of the mind, namely, obedience to God in singleness of heart, and in the practice of justice and charity; and I further point out, that this doctrine is set forth in Scripture in accordance with the opinions and understandings of those, among whom the Apostles and Prophets preached, to the end that men might receive it willingly, and with their whole heart.

(45) Having thus laid bare the bases of belief, I draw the conclusion that Revelation has obedience for its sole object, therefore, in purpose no less than in foundation and method, stands entirely aloof from ordinary knowledge; each has its separate province, neither can be called the handmaid of the other.

(46) Furthermore, as men's habits of mind differ, so that some more readily embrace one form of faith, some another, for what moves one to pray may move another only to scoff, I conclude, in accordance with what has gone before, that everyone should be free to choose for himself the foundations of his creed, and that faith should be judged only by its fruits; each would then obey God freely with his whole heart, while nothing would be publicly honoured save justice and charity.

(47) Having thus drawn attention to the liberty conceded to everyone by the revealed law of God, I pass on to another part of my subject, and prove that this same liberty can and should be accorded with safety to the state and the magisterial authority - in fact, that it cannot be withheld without great danger to peace and detriment to the community.

(48) In order to establish my point, I start from the natural rights of the individual, which are co-extensive with his desires and power, and from the fact that no one is bound to live as another pleases, but is the guardian of his own liberty. (49) I show that these rights can only be transferred to those whom we depute to defend us, who acquire with the duties of defence the power of ordering our lives, and I thence infer that rulers possess rights only limited by their power, that they are the sole guardians of justice and liberty, and that their subjects should act in all things as they dictate: nevertheless, since no one can so utterly abdicate his own power of self-defence as to cease to be a man, I conclude that no one can be deprived of his natural rights absolutely, but that subjects, either by tacit agreement, or by social contract, retain a certain number, which cannot be taken from them without great danger to the state.

(50) From these considerations I pass on to the Hebrew State, which I describe at some length, in order to trace the manner in which Religion acquired the force of law, and to touch on other noteworthy points. (51) I then prove, that the holders of sovereign power are the depositories and interpreters of religious no less than of civil ordinances, and that they alone have the right to

decide what is just or unjust, pious or impious; lastly, I conclude by showing, that they best retain this right and secure safety to their state by allowing every man to think what he likes, and say what he thinks.

(52) Such, Philosophical Reader, are the questions I submit to your notice, counting on your approval, for the subject matter of the whole book and of the several chapters is important and profitable. (53) I would say more, but I do not want my preface to extend to a volume, especially as I know that its leading propositions are to Philosophers but common places. (54) To the rest of mankind I care not to commend my treatise, for I cannot expect that it contains anything to please them: I know how deeply rooted are the prejudices embraced under the name of religion; I am aware that in the mind of the masses superstition is no less deeply rooted than fear; I recognize that their constancy is mere obstinacy, and that they are led to praise or blame by impulse rather than reason. (55) Therefore the multitude, and those of like passions with the multitude, I ask not to read my book; nay, I would rather that they should utterly neglect it, than that they should misinterpret it after their wont. (56) They would gain no good themselves, and might prove a stumbling-block to others, whose philosophy is hampered by the belief that Reason is a mere handmaid to Theology, and whom I seek in this work especially to benefit. (57) But as there will be many who have neither the leisure, nor, perhaps, the inclination to read through all I have written, I feel bound here, as at the end of my treatise, to declare that I have written nothing, which I do not most willingly submit to the examination and judgment of my country's rulers, and that I am ready to retract anything, which they shall decide to be repugnant to the laws or prejudicial to the public good. (58) I know that I am a man and, as a man, liable to error, but against error I have taken scrupulous care, and striven to keep in entire accordance with the laws of my country, with loyalty, and with morality.

CHAPTER I. - Of Prophecy

(1) Prophecy, or revelation is sure knowledge revealed by God to man. (2) A prophet is one who interprets the revelations of God {insights} to those who are unable to attain to sure knowledge of the matters revealed, and therefore can only apprehend them by simple faith.

(3) The Hebrew word for prophet is "naw-vee'", Strong:5030, [Endnote 1] i.e. speaker or interpreter, but in Scripture its meaning is restricted to interpreter of God, as we may learn from Exodus vii:1, where God says to Moses, "See, I have made thee a god to Pharaoh, and Aaron thy brother shall be thy prophet;" implying that, since in interpreting Moses' words to Pharaoh, Aaron acted the part of a prophet, Moses would be to Pharaoh as a god, or in the attitude of a god.

(4) Prophets I will treat of in the next chapter, and at present consider prophecy.

(5) Now it is evident, from the definition above given, that prophecy really includes ordinary knowledge; for the knowledge which we acquire by our natural faculties depends on knowledge of God and His eternal laws; but ordinary knowledge is common to all men as men, and rests on foundations which all share, whereas the multitude always strains after rarities and exceptions, and thinks little of the gifts of nature; so that, when prophecy is talked of, ordinary knowledge is not supposed to be included. (6) Nevertheless it has as much right as any other to be called Divine, for God's nature, in so far as we share therein, and God's laws, dictate it to us; nor does it suffer from that to which we give the preeminence, except in so far as the latter transcends its limits and cannot be accounted for by natural laws taken in themselves. (7) In respect to the certainty it involves, and the source from which it is derived, i.e. God, ordinary, knowledge is no whit inferior to prophetic, unless indeed we believe, or rather dream, that the prophets had human bodies but superhuman minds, and therefore that their sensations and consciousness were entirely different from our own.

(8) But, although ordinary knowledge is Divine, its professors cannot be called prophets [Endnote 2], for they teach what the rest of mankind could perceive and apprehend, not merely by simple faith, but as surely and honourably as themselves.

(9) Seeing then that our mind subjectively contains in itself and partakes of the nature of God, and solely from this cause is enabled to form notions explaining natural phenomena and inculcating morality, it follows that we may rightly assert the nature of the human mind (in so far as it is thus conceived) to be a primary cause of Divine revelation. (10) All that we clearly and distinctly understand is dictated to us, as I have just pointed out, by the idea and nature of God; not indeed through words, but in a way far more excellent and agreeing perfectly with the nature of the mind, as all who have enjoyed intellectual certainty will doubtless attest. (11) Here, however, my chief purpose is to speak of matters having reference to Scripture, so these few words on the light of reason will suffice.

(12) I will now pass on to, and treat more fully, the other ways and means by which God makes revelations to mankind, both of that which transcends ordinary knowledge, and of that within its scope; for there is no reason why God should not employ other means to communicate what we

know already by the power of reason.

(13) Our conclusions on the subject must be drawn solely from Scripture; for what can we affirm about matters transcending our knowledge except what is told us by the words or writings of prophets? (14) And since there are, so far as I know, no prophets now alive, we have no alternative but to read the books of prophets departed, taking care the while not to reason from metaphor or to ascribe anything to our authors which they do not themselves distinctly state. (15) I must further premise that the Jews never make any mention or account of secondary, or particular causes, but in a spirit of religion, piety, and what is commonly called godliness, refer all things directly to the Deity. (16) For instance if they make money by a transaction, they say God gave it to them; if they desire anything, they say God has disposed their hearts towards it; if they think anything, they say God told them. (17) Hence we must not suppose that everything is prophecy or revelation which is described in Scripture as told by God to anyone, but only such things as are expressly announced as prophecy or revelation, or are plainly pointed to as such by the context.

(18) A perusal of the sacred books will show us that all God's revelations to the prophets were made through words or appearances, or a combination of the two. (19) These words and appearances were of two kinds; 1.- real when external to the mind of the prophet who heard or saw them, 2.- imaginary when the imagination of the prophet was in a state which led him distinctly to suppose that he heard or saw them.

(20) With a real voice God revealed to Moses the laws which He wished to be transmitted to the Hebrews, as we may see from Exodus xxv:22, where God says, "And there I will meet with thee and I will commune with thee from the mercy seat which is between the Cherubim." (21) Some sort of real voice must necessarily have been employed, for Moses found God ready to commune with him at any time. This, as I shall shortly show, is the only instance of a real voice.

(22) We might, perhaps, suppose that the voice with which God called Samuel was real, for in 1 Sam. iii:21, we read, "And the Lord appeared again in Shiloh, for the Lord revealed Himself to Samuel in Shiloh by the word of the Lord;" implying that the appearance of the Lord consisted in His making Himself known to Samuel through a voice; in other words, that Samuel heard the Lord speaking. (23) But we are compelled to distinguish between the prophecies of Moses and those of other prophets, and therefore must decide that this voice was imaginary, a conclusion further supported by the voice's resemblance to the voice of Eli, which Samuel was in the habit of hearing, and therefore might easily imagine; when thrice called by the Lord, Samuel supposed it to have been Eli.

(24) The voice which Abimelech heard was imaginary, for it is written, Gen. xx:6, "And God said unto him in a dream." (25) So that the will of God was manifest to him, not in waking, but only, in sleep, that is, when the imagination is most active and uncontrolled. (26) Some of the Jews believe that the actual words of the Decalogue were not spoken by God, but that the Israelites heard a noise only, without any distinct words, and during its continuance apprehended the Ten Commandments by pure intuition; to this opinion I myself once inclined, seeing that the words of the Decalogue in Exodus are different from the words of the Decalogue in

Deuteronomy, for the discrepancy seemed to imply (since God only spoke once) that the Ten Commandments were not intended to convey the actual words of the Lord, but only His meaning. (27) However, unless we would do violence to Scripture, we must certainly admit that the Israelites heard a real voice, for Scripture expressly says, Deut. v:4, "God spake with you face to face," i.e. as two men ordinarily interchange ideas through the instrumentality of their two bodies; and therefore it seems more consonant with Holy Writ to suppose that God really did create a voice of some kind with which the Decalogue was revealed. (28) The discrepancy of the two versions is treated of in Chap. VIII.

(29) Yet not even thus is all difficulty removed, for it seems scarcely reasonable to affirm that a created thing, depending on God in the same manner as other created things, would be able to express or explain the nature of God either verbally or really by means of its individual organism: for instance, by declaring in the first person, "I am the Lord your God."

(30) Certainly when anyone says with his mouth, "I understand," we do not attribute the understanding to the mouth, but to the mind of the speaker; yet this is because the mouth is the natural organ of a man speaking, and the hearer, knowing what understanding is, easily comprehends, by a comparison with himself, that the speaker's mind is meant; but if we knew nothing of God beyond the mere name and wished to commune with Him, and be assured of His existence, I fail to see how our wish would be satisfied by the declaration of a created thing (depending on God neither more nor less than ourselves), "I am the Lord." (31) If God contorted the lips of Moses, or, I will not say Moses, but some beast, till they pronounced the words, "I am the Lord," should we apprehend the Lord's existence therefrom?

(32) Scripture seems clearly to point to the belief that God spoke Himself, having descended from heaven to Mount Sinai for the purpose - and not only that the Israelites heard Him speaking, but that their chief men beheld Him (Ex:xxiv.) (33) Further the law of Moses, which might neither be added to nor curtailed, and which was set up as a national standard of right, nowhere prescribed the belief that God is without body, or even without form or figure, but only ordained that the Jews should believe in His existence and worship Him alone: it forbade them to invent or fashion any likeness of the Deity, but this was to insure purity of service; because, never having seen God, they could not by means of images recall the likeness of God, but only the likeness of some created thing which might thus gradually take the place of God as the object of their adoration. (34) Nevertheless, the Bible clearly implies that God has a form, and that Moses when he heard God speaking was permitted to behold it, or at least its hinder parts.

(35) Doubtless some mystery lurks in this question which we will discuss more fully below. (36) For the present I will call attention to the passages in Scripture indicating the means by which God has revealed His laws to man.

(37) Revelation may be through figures only, as in I Chron:xxii., where God displays his anger to David by means of an angel bearing a sword, and also in the story of Balaam.

(38) Maimonides and others do indeed maintain that these and every other instance of angelic apparitions (e.g. to Manoah and to Abraham offering up Isaac) occurred during sleep, for that no one with his eyes open ever could see an angel, but this is mere nonsense. (39) The sole object of

such commentators seems to be to extort from Scripture confirmations of Aristotelian quibbles and their own inventions, a proceeding which I regard as the acme of absurdity.

(40) In figures, not real but existing only in the prophet's imagination, God revealed to Joseph his future lordship, and in words and figures He revealed to Joshua that He would fight for the Hebrews, causing to appear an angel, as it were the Captain of the Lord's host, bearing a sword, and by this means communicating verbally. (41) The forsaking of Israel by Providence was portrayed to Isaiah by a vision of the Lord, the thrice Holy, sitting on a very lofty throne, and the Hebrews, stained with the mire of their sins, sunk as it were in uncleanness, and thus as far as possible distant from God. (42) The wretchedness of the people at the time was thus revealed, while future calamities were foretold in words. I could cite from Holy Writ many similar examples, but I think they are sufficiently well known already.

(43) However, we get a still more clear confirmation of our position in Num xii:6,7, as follows: "If there be any prophet among you, I the Lord will make myself known unto him in a vision" (i.e. by appearances and signs, for God says of the prophecy of Moses that it was a vision without signs), "and will speak unto him in a dream" (i.e. not with actual words and an actual voice). (44) "My servant Moses is not so; with him will I speak mouth to mouth, even apparently, and not in dark speeches, and the similitude of the Lord he shall behold," i.e. looking on me as a friend and not afraid, he speaks with me (cf. Ex xxxiii:17).

(45) This makes it indisputable that the other prophets did not hear a real voice, and we gather as much from Deut. xxiv:10: "And there arose not a prophet since in Israel like unto Moses whom the Lord knew face to face," which must mean that the Lord spoke with none other; for not even Moses saw the Lord's face. (46) These are the only media of communication between God and man which I find mentioned in Scripture, and therefore the only ones which may be supposed or invented. (47) We may be able quite to comprehend that God can communicate immediately with man, for without the intervention of bodily means He communicates to our minds His essence; still, a man who can by pure intuition comprehend ideas which are neither contained in nor deducible from the foundations of our natural knowledge, must necessarily possess a mind far superior to those of his fellow men, nor do I believe that any have been so endowed save Christ. (48) To Him the ordinances of God leading men to salvation were revealed directly without words or visions, so that God manifested Himself to the Apostles through the mind of Christ as He formerly did to Moses through the supernatural voice. (49) In this sense the voice of Christ, like the voice which Moses heard, may be called the voice of God, and it may be said that the wisdom of God (i.e. wisdom more than human) took upon itself in Christ human nature, and that Christ was the way of salvation. (50) I must at this juncture declare that those doctrines which certain churches put forward concerning Christ, I neither affirm nor deny, for I freely confess that I do not understand them. (51) What I have just stated I gather from Scripture, where I never read that God appeared to Christ, or spoke to Christ, but that God was revealed to the Apostles through Christ; that Christ was the Way of Life, and that the old law was given through an angel, and not immediately by God; whence it follows that if Moses spoke with God face to face as a man speaks with his friend (i.e. by means of their two bodies) Christ communed

with God mind to mind.

(52) Thus we may conclude that no one except Christ received the revelations of God without the aid of imagination, whether in words or vision. (53) Therefore the power of prophecy implies not a peculiarly perfect mind, but a peculiarly vivid imagination, as I will show more clearly in the next chapter. (54) We will now inquire what is meant in the Bible by the Spirit of God breathed into the prophets, or by the prophets speaking with the Spirit of God; to that end we must determine the exact signification of the Hebrew word roo'-akh, Strong:7307, commonly translated spirit.

(55) The word roo'-akh, Strong:7307, literally means a wind, e..q. the south wind, but it is frequently employed in other derivative significations.

It is used as equivalent to,

(56) (1.) Breath: "Neither is there any spirit in his mouth," Ps. cxxxv:17.

(57) (2.) Life, or breathing: "And his spirit returned to him" 1 Sam. xxx:12; i.e. he breathed again.

(58) (3.) Courage and strength: "Neither did there remain any more spirit in any man," Josh. ii:11; "And the spirit entered into me, and made me stand on my feet," Ezek. ii:2.

(59) (4.) Virtue and fitness: "Days should speak, and multitudes of years should teach wisdom; but there is a spirit in man," Job xxxii:7; i.e. wisdom is not always found among old men for I now discover that it depends on individual virtue and capacity. So, "A man in whom is the Spirit," Numbers xxvii:18.

(60) (5.) Habit of mind: "Because he had another spirit with him," Numbers xiv:24; i.e. another habit of mind. "Behold I will pour out My Spirit unto you," Prov. i:23.

(61) (6.) Will, purpose, desire, impulse: "Whither the spirit was to go, they went," Ezek. 1:12; "That cover with a covering, but not of My Spirit," Is. xxx:1; "For the Lord hath poured out on you the spirit of deep sleep," Is. xxix:10; "Then was their spirit softened," Judges viii:3; "He that ruleth his spirit, is better than he that taketh a city," Prov. xvi:32; "He that hath no ru over his own spirit," Prov. xxv:28; "Your spirit as fire shall devour you," Isaiah xxxiii:1.

From the meaning of disposition we get -

(62) (7.) Passions and faculties. A lofty spirit means pride, a lowly spirit humility, an evil spirit hatred and melancholy. So, too, the expressions spirits of jealousy, fornication, wisdom, counsel, bravery, stand for a jealous, lascivious, wise, prudent, or brave mind (for we Hebrews use substantives in preference to adjectives), or these various qualities.

(63) (8.) The mind itself, or the life: "Yea, they have all one spirit," Eccles. iii:19 "The spirit shall return to God Who gave it."

(64) (9.) The quarters of the world (from the winds which blow thence), or even the side of anything turned towards a particular quarter - Ezek. xxxvii:9; xlii:16, 17, 18, 19, &c.

(65) I have already alluded to the way in which things are referred to God, and said to be of God.

(66) (1.) As belonging to His nature, and being, as it were, part of Him; e.g. the power of God, the eyes of God.

(67) (2.) As under His dominion, and depending on His pleasure; thus the heavens are called the heavens of the Lord, as being His chariot and habitation. So Nebuchadnezzar is called the servant of God, Assyria the scourge of God, &c.

(68) (3.) As dedicated to Him, e.g. the Temple of God, a Nazarene of God, the Bread of God.

(69) (4.) As revealed through the prophets and not through our natural faculties. In this sense the Mosaic law is called the law of God.

(70) (5.) As being in the superlative degree. Very high mountains are styled the mountains of God, a very deep sleep, the sleep of God, &c. In this sense we must explain Amos iv:11: "I have overthrown you as the overthrow of the Lord came upon Sodom and Gomorrah," i.e. that memorable overthrow, for since God Himself is the Speaker, the passage cannot well be taken otherwise. The wisdom of Solomon is called the wisdom of God, or extraordinary. The size of the cedars of Lebanon is alluded to in the Psalmist's expression, "the cedars of the Lord."

(71) Similarly, if the Jews were at a loss to understand any phenomenon, or were ignorant of its cause, they referred it to God. (72) Thus a storm was termed the chiding of God, thunder and lightning the arrows of God, for it was thought that God kept the winds confined in caves, His treasuries; thus differing merely in name from the Greek wind-god Eolus. (73) In like manner miracles were called works of God, as being especially marvellous; though in reality, of course, all natural events are the works of God, and take place solely by His power. (74) The Psalmist calls the miracles in Egypt the works of God, because the Hebrews found in them a way of safety which they had not looked for, and therefore especially marvelled at.

(75) As, then, unusual natural phenomena are called works of God, and trees of unusual size are called trees of God, we cannot wonder that very strong and tall men, though impious robbers and whoremongers, are in Genesis called sons of God.

(76) This reference of things wonderful to God was not peculiar to the Jews.

(77) Pharaoh, on hearing the interpretation of his dream, exclaimed that the mind of the gods was in Joseph. (78) Nebuchadnezzar told Daniel that he possessed the mind of the holy gods; so also in Latin anything well made is often said to be wrought with Divine hands, which is equivalent to the Hebrew phrase, wrought with the hand of God.

(80) We can now very easily understand and explain those passages of Scripture which speak of the Spirit of God. (81) In some places the expression merely means a very strong, dry, and deadly wind, as in Isaiah xl:7, "The grass withereth, the flower fadeth, because the Spirit of the Lord bloweth upon it." (82) Similarly in Gen. i:2: "The Spirit of the Lord moved over the face of the waters." (83) At other times it is used as equivalent to a high courage, thus the spirit of Gideon and of Samson is called the Spirit of the Lord, as being very bold, and prepared for any emergency. (84) Any unusual virtue or power is called the Spirit or Virtue of the Lord, Ex. xxxi:3: "I will fill him (Bezaleel) with the Spirit of the Lord," i.e., as the Bible itself explains, with talent above man's usual endowment. (85) So Isa. xi:2: "And the Spirit of the Lord shall rest upon him," is explained afterwards in the text to mean the spirit of wisdom and understanding, of counsel and might.

(86) The melancholy of Saul is called the melancholy of the Lord, or a very deep melancholy,

the persons who applied the term showing that they understood by it nothing supernatural, in that they sent for a musician to assuage it by harp-playing. (87) Again, the "Spirit of the Lord" is used as equivalent to the mind of man, for instance, Job xxvii:3: "And the Spirit of the Lord in my nostrils," the allusion being to Gen. ii:7: "And God breathed into man's nostrils the breath of life." (88) Ezekiel also, prophesying to the dead, says (xxvii:14), "And I will give to you My Spirit, and ye shall live;" i.e. I will restore you to life. (89) In Job xxxiv:14, we read: "If He gather unto Himself His Spirit and breath;" in Gen. vi:3: "My Spirit shall not always strive with man, for that he also is flesh," i.e. since man acts on the dictates of his body, and not the spirit which I gave him to discern the good, I will let him alone. (90) So, too, Ps. li:12: "Create in me a clean heart, 0 God, and renew a right spirit within me; cast me not away from Thy presence, and take not Thy Holy Spirit from me." (91) It was supposed that sin originated only from the body, and that good impulses come from the mind; therefore the Psalmist invokes the aid of God against the bodily appetites, but prays that the spirit which the Lord, the Holy One, had given him might be renewed. (92) Again, inasmuch as the Bible, in concession to popular ignorance, describes God as having a mind, a heart, emotions - nay, even a body and breath - the expression Spirit of the Lord is used for God's mind, disposition, emotion, strength, or breath. (93) Thus, Isa. xl:13: "Who hath disposed the Spirit of the Lord?" i.e. who, save Himself, hath caused the mind of the Lord to will anything,? and Isa. lxiii:10: "But they rebelled, and vexed the Holy Spirit."

(94) The phrase comes to be used of the law of Moses, which in a sense expounds God's will, Is. lxiii. 11, "Where is He that put His Holy Spirit within him?" meaning, as we clearly gather from the context, the law of Moses. (95) Nehemiah, speaking of the giving of the law, says, i:20, "Thou gavest also thy good Spirit to instruct them." (96) This is referred to in Deut. iv:6, "This is your wisdom and understanding," and in Ps. cxliii:10, "Thy good Spirit will lead me into the land of uprightness." (97) The Spirit of the Lord may mean the breath of the Lord, for breath, no less than a mind, a heart, and a body are attributed to God in Scripture, as in Ps. xxxiii:6. (98) Hence it gets to mean the power, strength, or faculty of God, as in Job xxxiii:4, "The Spirit of the Lord made me," i.e. the power, or, if you prefer, the decree of the Lord. (99) So the Psalmist in poetic language declares, xxxiii:6, "By the word of the Lord were the heavens made, and all the host of them by the breath of His mouth," i.e. by a mandate issued, as it were, in one breath. (100) Also Ps. cxxxix:7, "Wither shall I go from Thy Spirit, or whither shall I flee from Thy presence?" i.e. whither shall I go so as to be beyond Thy power and Thy presence?

(101) Lastly, the Spirit of the Lord is used in Scripture to express the emotions of God, e.g. His kindness and mercy, Micah ii:7, "Is the Spirit [i.e. the mercy] of the Lord straitened? (102) Are these cruelties His doings?" (103) Zech. iv:6, "Not by might or by power, but My Spirit [i.e. mercy], saith the Lord of hosts." (104) The twelfth verse of the seventh chapter of the same prophet must, I think, be interpreted in like manner: "Yea, they made their hearts as an adamant stone, lest they should hear the law, and the words which the Lord of hosts hath sent in His Spirit [i.e. in His mercy] by the former prophets." (105) So also Haggai ii:5: "So My Spirit remaineth among you: fear not."

(106) The passage in Isaiah xlviii:16, "And now the Lord and His Spirit hath sent me," may be taken to refer to God's mercy or His revealed law; for the prophet says, "From the beginning" (i.e. from the time when I first came to you, to preach God's anger and His sentence forth against you) "I spoke not in secret; from the time that it was, there am I," and now I am sent by the mercy of God as a joyful messenger to preach your restoration. (107) Or we may understand him to mean by the revealed law that he had before come to warn them by the command of the law (Levit. xix:17) in the same manner under the same conditions as Moses had warned them, that now, like Moses, he ends by preaching their restoration. (108) But the first explanation seems to me the best.

(109) Returning, then, to the main object of our discussion, we find that the Scriptural phrases, "The Spirit of the Lord was upon a prophet," "The Lord breathed His Spirit into men," "Men were filled with the Spirit of God, with the Holy Spirit," &c., are quite clear to us, and mean that prophets were endowed with a peculiar and extraordinary power, and devoted themselves to piety with especial constancy(3); that thus they perceived the mind or the thought of God, for we have shown that God's Spirit signifies in Hebrew God's mind or thought, and that the law which shows His mind and thought is called His Spirit; hence that the imagination of the prophets, inasmuch as through it were revealed the decrees of God, may equally be called the mind of God, and the prophets be said to have possessed the mind of God. (110) On our minds also the mind of God and His eternal thoughts are impressed; but this being the same for all men is less taken into account, especially by the Hebrews, who claimed a pre-eminence, and despised other men and other men's knowledge.

(111) Lastly, the prophets were said to possess the Spirit of God because men knew not the cause of prophetic knowledge, and in their wonder referred it with other marvels directly to the Deity, styling it Divine knowledge.

(112) We need no longer scruple to affirm that the prophets only perceived God's revelation by the aid of imagination, that is, by words and figures either real or imaginary. (113) We find no other means mentioned in Scripture, and therefore must not invent any. (114) As to the particular law of Nature by which the communications took place, I confess my ignorance. (115) I might, indeed, say as others do, that they took place by the power of God; but this would be mere trifling, and no better than explaining some unique specimen by a transcendental term. (116) Everything takes place by the power of God. (117) Nature herself is the power of God under another name, and our ignorance of the power of God is co-extensive with our ignorance of Nature. (118) It is absolute folly, therefore, to ascribe an event to the power of God when we know not its natural cause, which is the power of God.

(119) However, we are not now inquiring into the causes of prophetic knowledge. (120) We are only attempting, as I have said, to examine the Scriptural documents, and to draw our conclusions from them as from ultimate natural facts; the causes of the documents do not concern us.

(121) As the prophets perceived the revelations of God by the aid of imagination, they could indisputably perceive much that is beyond the boundary of the intellect, for many more ideas can

be constructed from words and figures than from the principles and notions on which the whole fabric of reasoned knowledge is reared.

(122) Thus we have a clue to the fact that the prophets perceived nearly everything in parables and allegories, and clothed spiritual truths in bodily forms, for such is the usual method of imagination. (122) We need no longer wonder that Scripture and the prophets speak so strangely and obscurely of God's Spirit or Mind (cf. Numbers xi:17, 1 Kings xxii:21, &c.), that the Lord was seen by Micah as sitting, by Daniel as an old man clothed in white, by Ezekiel as a fire, that the Holy Spirit appeared to those with Christ as a descending dove, to the apostles as fiery tongues, to Paul on his conversion as a great light. (124) All these expressions are plainly in harmony with the current ideas of God and spirits.

(125) Inasmuch as imagination is fleeting and inconstant, we find that the power of prophecy did not remain with a prophet for long, nor manifest itself frequently, but was very rare; manifesting itself only in a few men, and in them not often.

(126) We must necessarily inquire how the prophets became assured of the truth of what they perceived by imagination, and not by sure mental laws; but our investigation must be confined to Scripture, for the subject is one on which we cannot acquire certain knowledge, and which we cannot explain by the immediate causes. (127) Scripture teaching about the assurance of prophets I will treat of in the next chapter.

CHAPTER II. - OF PROPHETS.

(1) It follows from the last chapter that, as I have said, the prophets were endowed with unusually vivid imaginations, and not with unusually, perfect minds. (2) This conclusion is amply sustained by Scripture, for we are told that Solomon was the wisest of men, but had no special faculty of prophecy. (3) Heman, Calcol, and Dara, though men of great talent, were not prophets, whereas uneducated countrymen, nay, even women, such as Hagar, Abraham's handmaid, were thus gifted. (4) Nor is this contrary to ordinary experience and reason. (5) Men of great imaginative power are less fitted for abstract reasoning, whereas those who excel in intellect and its use keep their imagination more restrained and controlled, holding it in subjection, so to speak, lest it should usurp the place of reason.

(6) Thus to suppose that knowledge of natural and spiritual phenomena can be gained from the prophetic books, is an utter mistake, which I shall endeavour to expose, as I think philosophy, the age, and the question itself demand. (7) I care not for the girdings of superstition, for superstition is the bitter enemy, of all true knowledge and true morality. (8) Yes; it has come to this! (9) Men who openly confess that they can form no idea of God, and only know Him through created things, of which they know not the causes, can unblushingly, accuse philosophers of Atheism. (10) Treating the question methodically, I will show that prophecies varied, not only according to the imagination and physical temperament of the prophet, but also according to his particular opinions; and further that prophecy never rendered the prophet wiser than he was before. (11) But I will first discuss the assurance of truth which the prophets received, for this is akin to the subject-matter of the chapter, and will serve to elucidate somewhat our present point.

(12) Imagination does not, in its own nature, involve any certainty of truth, such as is implied in every clear and distinct idea, but requires some extrinsic reason to assure us of its objective reality: hence prophecy cannot afford certainty, and the prophets were assured of God's revelation by some sign, and not by the fact of revelation, as we may see from Abraham, who, when he had heard the promise of God, demanded a sign, not because he did not believe in God, but because he wished to be sure that it was God Who made the promise. (13) The fact is still more evident in the case of Gideon: "Show me," he says to God, "show me a sign, that I may know that it is Thou that talkest with me." (14) God also says to Moses: "And let this be a sign that I have sent thee." (15) Hezekiah, though he had long known Isaiah to be a prophet, none the less demanded a sign of the cure which he predicted. (15) It is thus quite evident that the prophets always received some sign to certify them of their prophetic imaginings; and for this reason Moses bids the Jews (Deut. xviii.) ask of the prophets a sign, namely, the prediction of some coming event. (16) In this respect, prophetic knowledge is inferior to natural knowledge, which needs no sign, and in itself implies certitude. (17) Moreover, Scripture warrants the statement that the certitude of the prophets was not mathematical, but moral. (18) Moses lays down the punishment of death for the prophet who preaches new gods, even though he confirm his doctrine by signs and wonders (Deut. xiii.); "For," he says, "the Lord also worketh signs and wonders to try His people." (19) And Jesus Christ warns His disciples of the same thing (Matt.

xxiv:24). (20) Furthermore, Ezekiel (xiv:9) plainly states that God sometimes deceives men with false revelations; and Micaiah bears like witness in the case of the prophets of Ahab.

(21) Although these instances go to prove that revelation is open to doubt, it nevertheless contains, as we have said, a considerable element of certainty, for God never deceives the good, nor His chosen, but (according to the ancient proverb, and as appears in the history of Abigail and her speech), God uses the good as instruments of goodness, and the wicked as means to execute His wrath. (22) This may be seen from the case of Micaiah above quoted; for although God had determined to deceive Ahab, through prophets, He made use of lying prophets; to the good prophet He revealed the truth, and did not forbid his proclaiming it.

(23) Still the certitude of prophecy, remains, as I have said, merely, moral; for no one can justify himself before God, nor boast that he is an instrument for God's goodness. (24) Scripture itself teaches and shows that God led away David to number the people, though it bears ample witness to David's piety.

(25) The whole question of the certitude of prophecy, was based on these three considerations:

1. That the things revealed were imagined very vividly, affecting the prophets in the same way as things seen when awake;

2. The presence of a sign;

3. Lastly, and chiefly, that the mind of the prophet was given wholly, to what was right and good.

(26) Although Scripture does not always make mention of a sign, we must nevertheless suppose that a sign was always vouchsafed; for Scripture does not always relate every condition and circumstance (as many, have remarked), but rather takes them for granted. (27) We may, however, admit that no sign was needed when the prophecy declared nothing that was not already contained in the law of Moses, because it was confirmed by that law. (28) For instance, Jeremiah's prophecy, of the destruction of Jerusalem was confirmed by the prophecies of other prophets, and by the threats in the law, and, therefore, it needed no sign; whereas Hananiah, who, contrary to all the prophets, foretold the speedy restoration of the state, stood in need of a sign, or he would have been in doubt as to the truth of his prophecy, until it was confirmed by facts. (29) "The prophet which prophesieth of peace, when the word of the prophet shall come to pass, then shall the prophet be known that the Lord hath truly sent him."

(30) As, then, the certitude afforded to the prophet by signs was not mathematical (i.e. did not necessarily follow from the perception of the thing perceived or seen), but only moral, and as the signs were only given to convince the prophet, it follows that such signs were given according to the opinions and capacity of each prophet, so that a sign which convince one prophet would fall far short of convincing another who was imbued with different opinions. (31) Therefore the signs varied according to the individual prophet.

(32) So also did the revelation vary, as we have stated, according to individual disposition and temperament, and according to the opinions previously held.

(33) It varied according to disposition, in this way: if a prophet was cheerful, victories, peace, and events which make men glad, were revealed to him; in that he was naturally more likely to

imagine such things. (34) If, on the contrary, he was melancholy, wars, massacres, and calamities were revealed; and so, according as a prophet was merciful, gentle, quick to anger, or severe, he was more fitted for one kind of revelation than another. (35) It varied according to the temper of imagination in this way: if a prophet was cultivated he perceived the mind of God in a cultivated way, if he was confused he perceived it confusedly. (36) And so with revelations perceived through visions. (37) If a prophet was a countryman he saw visions of oxen, cows, and the like; if he was a soldier, he saw generals and armies; if a courtier, a royal throne, and so on.

(38) Lastly, prophecy varied according to the opinions held by the prophets; for instance, to the Magi, who believed in the follies of astrology, the birth of Christ was revealed through the vision of a star in the East. (39) To the augurs of Nebuchadnezzar the destruction of Jerusalem was revealed through entrails, whereas the king himself inferred it from oracles and the direction of arrows which he shot into the air. (40) To prophets who believed that man acts from free choice and by his own power, God was revealed as standing apart from and ignorant of future human actions. (41) All of which we will illustrate from Scripture.

(42) The first point is proved from the case of Elisha, who, in order to prophecy to Jehoram, asked for a harp, and was unable to perceive the Divine purpose till he had been recreated by its music; then, indeed, he prophesied to Jehoram and to his allies glad tidings, which previously he had been unable to attain to because he was angry with the king, and these who are angry with anyone can imagine evil of him, but not good. (43) The theory that God does not reveal Himself to the angry or the sad, is a mere dream: for God revealed to Moses while angry, the terrible slaughter of the firstborn, and did so without the intervention of a harp. (44) To Cain in his rage, God was revealed, and to Ezekiel, impatient with anger, was revealed the contumacy and wretchedness of the Jews. (45) Jeremiah, miserable and weary of life, prophesied the disasters of the Hebrews, so that Josiah would not consult him, but inquired of a woman, inasmuch as it was more in accordance with womanly nature that God should reveal His mercy thereto. (46) So, Micaiah never prophesied good to Ahab, though other true prophets had done so, but invariably evil. (46) Thus we see that individual prophets were by temperament more fitted for one sort of revelation than another.

(47) The style of the prophecy also varied according to the eloquence of the individual prophet. (48) The prophecies of Ezekiel and Amos are not written in a cultivated style like those of Isaiah and Nahum, but more rudely. (49) Any Hebrew scholar who wishes to inquire into this point more closely, and compares chapters of the different prophets treating of the same subject, will find great dissimilarity of style. (50) Compare, for instance, chap. i. of the courtly Isaiah, verse 11 to verse 20, with chap. v. of the countryman Amos, verses 21-24. (51) Compare also the order and reasoning of the prophecies of Jeremiah, written in Idumaea (chap. xlix.), with the order and reasoning of Obadiah. (52) Compare, lastly, Isa. xl:19, 20, and xliv:8, with Hosea viii:6, and xiii:2. And so on.

(53) A due consideration of these passage will clearly show us that God has no particular style in speaking, but, according to the learning and capacity of the prophet, is cultivated, compressed, severe, untutored, prolix, or obscure.

(54) There was, moreover, a certain variation in the visions vouchsafed to the prophets, and in the symbols by which they expressed them, for Isaiah saw the glory of the Lord departing from the Temple in a different form from that presented to Ezekiel. (55) The Rabbis, indeed, maintain that both visions were really the same, but that Ezekiel, being a countryman, was above measure impressed by it, and therefore set it forth in full detail; but unless there is a trustworthy tradition on the subject, which I do not for a moment believe, this theory is plainly an invention. Isaiah saw seraphim with six wings, Ezekiel beasts with four wings; Isaiah saw God clothed and sitting on a royal throne, Ezekiel saw Him in the likeness of a fire; each doubtless saw God under the form in which he usually imagined Him.

(56) Further, the visions varied in clearness as well as in details; for the revelations of Zechariah were too obscure to be understood by the prophet without explanation, as appears from his narration of them; the visions of Daniel could not be understood by him even after they had been explained, and this obscurity did not arise from the difficulty of the matter revealed (for being merely human affairs, these only transcended human capacity in being future), but solely in the fact that Daniel's imagination was not so capable for prophecy while he was awake as while he was asleep; and this is further evident from the fact that at the very beginning of the vision he was so terrified that he almost despaired of his strength. (57) Thus, on account of the inadequacy of his imagination and his strength, the things revealed were so obscure to him that he could not understand them even after they had been explained. (58) Here we may note that the words heard by Daniel, were, as we have shown above, simply imaginary, so that it is hardly wonderful that in his frightened state he imagined them so confusedly and obscurely that afterwards he could make nothing of them. (59) Those who say that God did not wish to make a clear revelation, do not seem to have read the words of the angel, who expressly says that he came to make the prophet understand what should befall his people in the latter days (Dan. x:14).

(60) The revelation remained obscure because no one was found, at that time, with imagination sufficiently strong to conceive it more clearly. (61) Lastly, the prophets, to whom it was revealed that God would take away Elijah, wished to persuade Elisha that he had been taken somewhere where they would find him; showing sufficiently clearly that they had not understood God's revelation aright.

(62) There is no need to set this out more amply, for nothing is more plain in the Bible than that God endowed some prophets with far greater gifts of prophecy than others. (63) But I will show in greater detail and length, for I consider the point more important, that the prophecies varied according to the opinions previously embraced by the prophets, and that the prophets held diverse and even contrary opinions and prejudices. (64) (I speak, be it understood, solely of matters speculative, for in regard to uprightness and morality the case is widely different.) (65) From thence I shall conclude that prophecy never rendered the prophets more learned, but left them with their former opinions, and that we are, therefore, not at all bound to trust them in matters of intellect.

(66) Everyone has been strangely hasty in affirming that the prophets knew everything within the scope of human intellect; and, although certain passages of Scripture plainly affirm that the

prophets were in certain respects ignorant, such persons would rather say that they do not understand the passages than admit that there was anything which the prophets did not know; or else they try to wrest the Scriptural words away from their evident meaning.

(67) If either of these proceedings is allowable we may as well shut our Bibles, for vainly shall we attempt to prove anything from them if their plainest passages may be classed among obscure and impenetrable mysteries, or if we may put any interpretation on them which we fancy. (68) For instance, nothing is more clear in the Bible than that Joshua, and perhaps also the author who wrote his history, thought that the sun revolves round the earth, and that the earth is fixed, and further that the sun for a certain period remained still. (69) Many, who will not admit any movement in the heavenly bodies, explain away the passage till it seems to mean something quite different; others, who have learned to philosophize more correctly, and understand that the earth moves while the sun is still, or at any rate does not revolve round the earth, try with all their might to wrest this meaning from Scripture, though plainly nothing of the sort is intended. (70) Such quibblers excite my wonder! (71) Are we, forsooth, bound to believe that Joshua the Soldier was a learned astronomer? or that a miracle could not be revealed to him, or that the light of the sun could not remain longer than usual above the horizon, without his knowing the cause? (72) To me both alternatives appear ridiculous, and therefore I would rather say, that Joshua was ignorant of the true cause of the lengthened day, and that he and the whole host with him thought that the sun moved round the earth every day, and that on that particular occasion it stood still for a time, thus causing the light to remain longer; and I would say, that they did not conjecture that, from the amount of snow in the air (see Josh. x:11), the refraction may have been greater than usual, or that there may have been some other cause which we will not now inquire into.

(73) So also the sign of the shadow going back was revealed to Isaiah according to his understanding; that is, as proceeding from a going backwards of the sun; for he, too, thought that the sun moves and that the earth is still; of parhelia he perhaps never even dreamed. (74) We may arrive at this conclusion without any, scruple, for the sign could really have come to pass, and have been predicted by Isaiah to the king, without the prophet being aware of the real cause.

(75) With regard to the building of the Temple by Solomon, if it was really dictate by God we must maintain the same doctrine: namely, that all the measurements were revealed according to the opinions and understanding of the king; for as we are not bound to believe that Solomon was a mathematician, we may affirm that he was ignorant of the true ratio between the circumference and the diameter of a circle, and that, like the generality of workmen, he thought that it was as three to one. (76) But if it is allowable to declare that we do not understand the passage, in good sooth I know nothing in the Bible that we can understand; for the process of building is there narrated simply and as a mere matter of history. (77) If, again, it is permitted to pretend that the passage has another meaning, and was written as it is from some reason unknown to us, this is no less than a complete subversal of the Bible; for every absurd and evil invention of human perversity could thus, without detriment to Scriptural authority, be defended and fostered. (78) Our conclusion is in no wise impious, for though Solomon, Isaiah, Joshua, &c. were prophets, they were none the less men, and as such not exempt from human shortcomings.

(79) According to the understanding of Noah it was revealed to him that God as about to destroy the whole human race, for Noah thought that beyond the limits of Palestine the world was not inhabited.

(80) Not only in matters of this kind, but in others more important, the about the Divine attributes, but held quite ordinary notions about God, and to these notions their revelations were adapted, as I will demonstrate by ample Scriptural testimony; from all which one may easily see that they were praised and commended, not so much for the sublimity and eminence of their intellect as for their piety and faithfulness.

(81) Adam, the first man to whom God was revealed, did not know that He is omnipotent and omniscient; for he hid himself from Him, and attempted to make excuses for his fault before God, as though he had had to do with a man; therefore to him also was God revealed according to his understanding - that is, as being unaware of his situation or his sin, for Adam heard, or seemed to hear, the Lord walling, in the garden, calling him and asking him where he was; and then, on seeing his shamefacedness, asking him whether he had eaten of the forbidden fruit. (82) Adam evidently only knew the Deity as the Creator of all things. (83) To Cain also God was revealed, according to his understanding, as ignorant of human affairs, nor was a higher conception of the Deity required for repentance of his sin.

(83) To Laban the Lord revealed Himself as the God of Abraham, because Laban believed that each nation had its own special divinity (see Gen. xxxi:29). (84) Abraham also knew not that God is omnipresent, and has foreknowledge of all things; for when he heard the sentence against the inhabitants of Sodom, he prayed that the Lord should not execute it till He had ascertained whether they all merited such punishment; for he said (see Gen. xviii:24), "Peradventure there be fifty righteous within the city," and in accordance with this belief God was revealed to him; as Abraham imagined, He spake thus: "I will go down now, and see whether they have done altogether according to the cry of it which is come unto Me; and, if not, I will know." (85) Further, the Divine testimony concerning Abraham asserts nothing but that he was obedient, and that he "commanded his household after him that they should keep the way of the Lord" (Gen. xviii:19); it does not state that he held sublime conceptions of the Deity.

(86) Moses, also, was not sufficiently aware that God is omniscient, and directs human actions by His sole decree, for although God Himself says that the Israelites should hearken to Him, Moses still considered the matter doubtful and repeated, "But if they will not believe me, nor hearken unto my voice." (87) To him in like manner God was revealed as taking no part in, and as being ignorant of, future human actions: the Lord gave him two signs and said, "And it shall come to pass that if they will not believe thee, neither hearken to the voice of the first sign, that they will believe the voice of the latter sign; but if not, thou shalt take of the water of the river," &c. (88) Indeed, if any one considers without prejudice the recorded opinions of Moses, he will plainly see that Moses conceived the Deity as a Being Who has always existed, does exist, and always will exist, and for this cause he calls Him by the name Jehovah, which in Hebrew signifies these three phases of existence: as to His nature, Moses only taught that He is merciful, gracious, and exceeding jealous, as appears from many passages in the Pentateuch. (89) Lastly,

he believed and taught that this Being was so different from all other beings, that He could not be expressed by the image of any visible thing; also, that He could not be looked upon, and that not so much from inherent impossibility as from human infirmity; further, that by reason of His power He was without equal and unique. (90) Moses admitted, indeed, that there were beings (doubtless by the plan and command of the Lord) who acted as God's vicegerents - that is, beings to whom God had given the right, authority, and power to direct nations, and to provide and care for them; but he taught that this Being Whom they were bound to obey was the highest and Supreme God, or (to use the Hebrew phrase) God of gods, and thus in the song (Exod. xv:11) he exclaims, "Who is like unto Thee, 0 Lord, among the gods?" and Jethro says (Exod. xviii:11), "Now I know that the Lord is greater than all gods." (91) That is to say, "I am at length compelled to admit to Moses that Jehovah is greater than all gods, and that His power is unrivalled." (92) We must remain in doubt whether Moses thought that these beings who acted as God's vicegerents were created by Him, for he has stated nothing, so far as we know, about their creation and origin. (93) He further taught that this Being had brought the visible world into order from Chaos, and had given Nature her germs, and therefore that He possesses supreme right and power over all things; further, that by reason of this supreme right and power He had chosen for Himself alone the Hebrew nation and a certain strip of territory, and had handed over to the care of other gods substituted by Himself the rest of the nations and territories, and that therefore He was called the God of Israel and the God of Jerusalem, whereas the other gods were called the gods of the Gentiles. (94) For this reason the Jews believed that the strip of territory which God had chosen for Himself, demanded a Divine worship quite apart and different from the worship which obtained elsewhere, and that the Lord would not suffer the worship of other gods adapted to other countries. (95) Thus they thought that the people whom the king of Assyria had brought into Judaea were torn in pieces by lions because they knew not the worship of the National Divinity (2 Kings xvii:25).

(96) Jacob, according to Aben Ezra's opinion, therefore admonished his sons when he wished them to seek out a new country, that they should prepare themselves for a new worship, and lay aside the worship of strange, gods - that is, of the gods of the land where they were (Gen. xxxv:2, 3).

(97) David, in telling Saul that he was compelled by the king's persecution to live away from his country, said that he was driven out from the heritage of the Lord, and sent to worship other gods (1 Sam. xxvi:19). (98) Lastly, he believed that this Being or Deity had His habitation in the heavens (Deut. xxxiii:27), an opinion very common among the Gentiles.

(99) If we now examine the revelations to Moses, we shall find that they were accommodated to these opinions; as he believed that the Divine Nature was subject to the conditions of mercy, graciousness, &c., so God was revealed to him in accordance with his idea and under these attributes (see Exodus xxxiv:6, 7, and the second commandment). (100) Further it is related (Ex. xxxiii:18) that Moses asked of God that he might behold Him, but as Moses (as we have said) had formed no mental image of God, and God (as I have shown) only revealed Himself to the prophets in accordance with the disposition of their imagination, He did not reveal Himself in

any form. (101) This, I repeat, was because the imagination of Moses was unsuitable, for other prophets bear witness that they saw the Lord; for instance, Isaiah, Ezekiel, Daniel, &c. (102) For this reason God answered Moses, "Thou canst not see My face;" and inasmuch as Moses believed that God can be looked upon - that is, that no contradiction of the Divine nature is therein involved (for otherwise he would never have preferred his request) - it is added, "For no one shall look on Me and live," thus giving a reason in accordance with Moses' idea, for it is not stated that a contradiction of the Divine nature would be involved, as was really the case, but that the thing would not come to pass because of human infirmity.

(103) When God would reveal to Moses that the Israelites, because they worshipped the calf, were to be placed in the same category as other nations, He said (ch. xxxiii:2, 3), that He would send an angel (that is, a being who should have charge of the Israelites, instead of the Supreme Being), and that He Himself would no longer remain among them; thus leaving Moses no ground for supposing that the Israelites were more beloved by God than the other nations whose guardianship He had entrusted to other beings or angels (vide verse 16).

(104) Lastly, as Moses believed that God dwelt in the heavens, God was revealed to him as coming down from heaven on to a mountain, and in order to talk with the Lord Moses went up the mountain, which he certainly need not have done if he could have conceived of God as omnipresent.

(105) The Israelites knew scarcely anything of God, although He was revealed to them; and this is abundantly evident from their transferring, a few days afterwards, the honour and worship due to Him to a calf, which they believed to be the god who had brought them out of Egypt. (106) In truth, it is hardly likely that men accustomed to the superstitions of Egypt, uncultivated and sunk in most abject slavery, should have held any sound notions about the Deity, or that Moses should have taught them anything beyond a rule of right living; inculcating it not like a philosopher, as the result of freedom, but like a lawgiver compelling them to be moral by legal authority. (107) Thus the rule of right living, the worship and love of God, was to them rather a bondage than the true liberty, the gift and grace of the Deity. (108) Moses bid them love God and keep His law, because they had in the past received benefits from Him (such as the deliverance from slavery in Egypt), and further terrified them with threats if they transgressed His commands, holding out many promises of good if they should observe them; thus treating them as parents treat irrational children. It is, therefore, certain that they knew not the excellence of virtue and the true happiness.

(109) Jonah thought that he was fleeing from the sight of God, which seems to show that he too held that God had entrusted the care of the nations outside Judaea to other substituted powers. (110) No one in the whole of the Old Testament speaks more rationally of God than Solomon, who in fact surpassed all the men of his time in natural ability. (111) Yet he considered himself above the law (esteeming it only to have been given for men without reasonable and intellectual grounds for their actions), and made small account of the laws concerning kings, which are mainly three: nay, he openly violated them (in this he did wrong, and acted in a manner unworthy of a philosopher, by indulging in sensual pleasure), and taught that all Fortune's

favours to mankind are vanity, that humanity has no nobler gift than wisdom, and no greater punishment than folly. (112) See Proverbs xvi:22, 23.

(113) But let us return to the prophets whose conflicting opinions we have undertaken to note. (114) The expressed ideas of Ezekiel seemed so diverse from those of Moses to the Rabbis who have left us the extant prophetic books (as is told in the treatise of Sabbathus, i:13, 2), that they had serious thoughts of omitting his prophecy from the canon, and would doubtless have thus excluded it if a certain Hananiah had not undertaken to explain it; a task which (as is there narrated) he with great zeal and labour accomplished. (115) How he did so does not sufficiently appear, whether it was by writing a commentary which has now perished, or by altering Ezekiel's words and audaciously - striking out phrases according to his fancy. (116) However this may be, chapter xviii. certainly does not seem to agree with Exodus xxxiv:7, Jeremiah xxxii:18, &c.

(117) Samuel believed that the Lord never repented of anything He had decreed (1 Sam. xv:29), for when Saul was sorry for his sin, and wished to worship God and ask for forgiveness, Samuel said that the Lord would not go back from his decree.

(118) To Jeremiah, on the other hand, it was revealed that, "If that nation against whom I (the Lord) have pronounced, turn from their evil, I will repent of the evil that I thought to do unto them. (119) If it do evil in my sight, that it obey not my voice, then I will repent of the good wherewith I said I would benefit them" (Jer. xviii:8-10). (120) Joel (ii:13) taught that the Lord repented Him only of evil. (121) Lastly, it is clear from Gen iv: 7 that a man can overcome the temptations of sin, and act righteously; for this doctrine is told to Cain, though, as we learn from Josephus and the Scriptures, he never did so overcome them. (122) And this agrees with the chapter of Jeremiah just cited, for it is there said that the Lord repents of the good or the evil pronounced, if the men in question change their ways and manner of life. (123) But, on the other hand, Paul (Rom.ix:10) teaches as plainly as possible that men have no control over the temptations of the flesh save by the special vocation and grace of God. (124) And when (Rom. iii:5 and vi:19) he attributes righteousness to man, he corrects himself as speaking merely humanly and through the infirmity of the flesh.

(125) We have now more than sufficiently proved our point, that God adapted revelations to the understanding and opinions of the prophets, and that in matters of theory without bearing on charity or morality the prophets could be, and, in fact, were, ignorant, and held conflicting opinions. (126) It therefore follows that we must by no means go to the prophets for knowledge, either of natural or of spiritual phenomena.

(127) We have determined, then, that we are only bound to believe in the prophetic writings, the object and substance of the revelation; with regard to the details, every one may believe or not, as he likes.

(128) For instance, the revelation to Cain only teaches us that God admonished him to lead the true life, for such alone is the object and substance of the revelation, not doctrines concerning free will and philosophy. (129) Hence, though the freedom of the will is clearly implied in the words of the admonition, we are at liberty to hold a contrary opinion, since the words and reasons were adapted to the understanding of Cain.

(130) So, too, the revelation to Micaiah would only teach that God revealed to him the true issue of the battle between Ahab and Aram; and this is all we are bound to believe. (131) Whatever else is contained in the revelation concerning the true and the false Spirit of God, the army of heaven standing on the right hand and on the left, and all the other details, does not affect us at all. (132) Everyone may believe as much of it as his reason allows.

(132) The reasonings by which the Lord displayed His power to Job (if they really were a revelation, and the author of the history is narrating, and not merely, as some suppose, rhetorically adorning his own conceptions), would come under the same category - that is, they were adapted to Job's understanding, for the purpose of convincing him, and are not universal, or for the convincing of all men.

(133) We can come to no different conclusion with respect to the reasonings of Christ, by which He convicted the Pharisees of pride and ignorance, and exhorted His disciples to lead the true life. (134) He adapted them to each man's opinions and principles. (135) For instance, when He said to the Pharisees (Matt. xii:26), "And if Satan cast out devils, his house is divided against itself, how then shall his kingdom stand? (136) "He only wished to convince the Pharisees according, to their own principles, not to teach that there are devils, or any kingdom of devils. (137) So, too, when He said to His disciples (Matt. viii:10), "See that ye despise not one of these little ones, for I say unto you that their angels," &c., He merely desired to warn them against pride and despising any of their fellows, not to insist on the actual reason given, which was simply adopted in order to persuade them more easily.

(138) Lastly, we should say, exactly the same of the apostolic signs and reasonings, but there is no need to go further into the subject. (139) If I were to enumerate all the passages of Scripture addressed only to individuals, or to a particular man's understanding, and which cannot, without great danger to philosophy, be defended as Divine doctrines, I should go far beyond the brevity at which I aim. (140) Let it suffice, then, to have indicated a few instances of general application, and let the curious reader consider others by himself. (141) Although the points we have just raised concerning prophets and prophecy are the only ones which have any direct bearing on the end in view, namely, the separation of Philosophy from Theology, still, as I have touched on the general question, I may here inquire whether the gift of prophecy was peculiar to the Hebrews, or whether it was common to all nations. (142) I must then come to a conclusion about the vocation of the Hebrews, all of which I shall do in the ensuing chapter.

CHAPTER III. OF THE VOCATION OF THE HEBREWS, AND WHETHER THE GIFT OF PROPHECY WAS PECULIAR TO THEM.

(1) Every man's true happiness and blessedness consist solely in the enjoyment of what is good, not in the pride that he alone is enjoying it, to the exclusion of others. (2) He who thinks himself the more blessed because he is enjoying benefits which others are not, or because he is more blessed or more fortunate than his fellows, is ignorant of true happiness and blessedness, and the joy which he feels is either childish or envious and malicious. (3) For instance, a man's true happiness consists only in wisdom, and the knowledge of the truth, not at all in the fact that he is wiser than others, or that others lack such knowledge: such considerations do not increase his wisdom or true happiness.

(4) Whoever, therefore, rejoices for such reasons, rejoices in another's misfortune, and is, so far, malicious and bad, knowing neither true happiness nor the peace of the true life.

(5) When Scripture, therefore, in exhorting the Hebrews to obey the law, says that the Lord has chosen them for Himself before other nations (Deut. x:15); that He is near them, but not near others (Deut. iv:7); that to them alone He has given just laws (Deut. iv:8); and, lastly, that He has marked them out before others (Deut. iv:32); it speaks only according to the understanding of its hearers, who, as we have shown in the last chapter, and as Moses also testifies (Deut. ix:6, 7), knew not true blessedness. (6) For in good sooth they would have been no less blessed if God had called all men equally to salvation, nor would God have been less present to them for being equally present to others; their laws, would have been no less just if they had been ordained for all, and they themselves would have been no less wise. (7) The miracles would have shown God's power no less by being wrought for other nations also; lastly, the Hebrews would have been just as much bound to worship God if He had bestowed all these gifts equally on all men.

(8) When God tells Solomon (1 Kings iii:12) that no one shall be as wise as he in time to come, it seems to be only a manner of expressing surpassing wisdom; it is little to be believed that God would have promised Solomon, for his greater happiness, that He would never endow anyone with so much wisdom in time to come; this would in no wise have increased Solomon's intellect, and the wise king would have given equal thanks to the Lord if everyone had been gifted with the same faculties.

(9) Still, though we assert that Moses, in the passages of the Pentateuch just cited, spoke only according to the understanding of the Hebrews, we have no wish to deny that God ordained the Mosaic law for them alone, nor that He spoke to them alone, nor that they witnessed marvels beyond those which happened to any other nation; but we wish to emphasize that Moses desired to admonish the Hebrews in such a manner, and with such reasonings as would appeal most forcibly to their childish understanding, and constrain them to worship the Deity. (10) Further, we wished to show that the Hebrews did not surpass other nations in knowledge, or in piety, but evidently in some attribute different from these; or (to speak like the Scriptures, according to their understanding), that the Hebrews were not chosen by God before others for the sake of the true life and sublime ideas, though they were often thereto admonished, but with some other

object. (11) What that object was, I will duly show.

(12) But before I begin, I wish in a few words to explain what I mean by the guidance of God, by the help of God, external and inward, and, lastly, what I understand by fortune.

(13) By the help of God, I mean the fixed and unchangeable order of nature or the chain of natural events: for I have said before and shown elsewhere that the universal laws of nature, according to which all things exist and are determined, are only another name for the eternal decrees of God, which always involve eternal truth and necessity.

(14) So that to say that everything happens according to natural laws, and to say that everything is ordained by the decree and ordinance of God, is the same thing. (15) Now since the power in nature is identical with the power of God, by which alone all things happen and are determined, it follows that whatsoever man, as a part of nature, provides himself with to aid and preserve his existence, or whatsoever nature affords him without his help, is given to him solely by the Divine power, acting either through human nature or through external circumstance. (16) So whatever human nature can furnish itself with by its own efforts to preserve its existence, may be fitly called the inward aid of God, whereas whatever else accrues to man's profit from outward causes may be called the external aid of God.

(17) We can now easily understand what is meant by the election of God. (18) For since no one can do anything save by the predetermined order of nature, that is by God's eternal ordinance and decree, it follows that no one can choose a plan of life for himself, or accomplish any work save by God's vocation choosing him for the work or the plan of life in question, rather than any other. (19) Lastly, by fortune, I mean the ordinance of God in so far as it directs human life through external and unexpected means. (20) With these preliminaries I return to my purpose of discovering the reason why the Hebrews were said to be elected by God before other nations, and with the demonstration I thus proceed.

(21) All objects of legitimate desire fall, generally speaking, under one of these three categories:

1. The knowledge of things through their primary causes.
2. The government of the passions, or the acquirement of the habit of virtue.
3. Secure and healthy life.

(22) The means which most directly conduce towards the first two of these ends, and which may be considered their proximate and efficient causes are contained in human nature itself, so that their acquisition hinges only on our own power, and on the laws of human nature. (23) It may be concluded that these gifts are not peculiar to any nation, but have always been shared by the whole human race, unless, indeed, we would indulge the dream that nature formerly created men of different kinds. (24) But the means which conduce to security and health are chiefly in external circumstance, and are called the gifts of fortune because they depend chiefly on objective causes of which we are ignorant; for a fool may be almost as liable to happiness or unhappiness as a wise man. (25) Nevertheless, human management and watchfulness can greatly assist towards living in security and warding off the injuries of our fellow-men, and even of beasts. (26) Reason and experience show no more certain means of attaining this object than the

formation of a society with fixed laws, the occupation of a strip of territory and the concentration of all forces, as it were, into one body, that is the social body. (27) Now for forming and preserving a society, no ordinary ability and care is required: that society will be most secure, most stable, and least liable to reverses, which is founded and directed by far-seeing and careful men; while, on the other hand, a society constituted by men without trained skill, depends in a great measure on fortune, and is less constant. (28) If, in spite of all, such a society lasts a long time, it is owing to some other directing influence than its own; if it overcomes great perils and its affairs prosper, it will perforce marvel at and adore the guiding Spirit of God (in so far, that is, as God works through hidden means, and not through the nature and mind of man), for everything happens to it unexpectedly and contrary to anticipation, it may even be said and thought to be by miracle. (29) Nations, then, are distinguished from one another in respect to the social organization and the laws under which they live and are governed; the Hebrew nation was not chosen by God in respect to its wisdom nor its tranquillity of mind, but in respect to its social organization and the good fortune with which it obtained supremacy and kept it so many years. (30) This is abundantly clear from Scripture. Even a cursory perusal will show us that the only respects in which the Hebrews surpassed other nations, are in their successful conduct of matters relating to government, and in their surmounting great perils solely by God's external aid; in other ways they were on a par with their fellows, and God was equally gracious to all. (31) For in respect to intellect (as we have shown in the last chapter) they held very ordinary ideas about God and nature, so that they cannot have been God's chosen in this respect; nor were they so chosen in respect of virtue and the true life, for here again they, with the exception of a very few elect, were on an equality with other nations: therefore their choice and vocation consisted only in the temporal happiness and advantages of independent rule. (32) In fact, we do not see that God promised anything beyond this to the patriarchs [Endnote 4] or their successors; in the law no other reward is offered for obedience than the continual happiness of an independent commonwealth and other goods of this life; while, on the other hand, against contumacy and the breaking of the covenant is threatened the downfall of the commonwealth and great hardships. (33) Nor is this to be wondered at; for the ends of every social organization and commonwealth are (as appears from what we have said, and as we will explain more at length hereafter) security and comfort; a commonwealth can only exist by the laws being binding on all. (34) If all the members of a state wish to disregard the law, by that very fact they dissolve the state and destroy the commonwealth. (35) Thus, the only reward which could be promised to the Hebrews for continued obedience to the law was security [Endnote 5] and its attendant advantages, while no surer punishment could be threatened for disobedience, than the ruin of the state and the evils which generally follow therefrom, in addition to such further consequences as might accrue to the Jews in particular from the ruin of their especial state. (36) But there is no need here to go into this point at more length. (37) I will only add that the laws of the Old Testament were revealed and ordained to the Jews only, for as God chose them in respect to the special constitution of their society and government, they must, of course, have had special laws. (38) Whether God ordained special laws for other nations also, and revealed Himself to their lawgivers prophetically, that is, under the attributes by which the latter were accustomed to imagine Him, I cannot sufficiently determine. (39) It is evident from Scripture itself that other nations acquired supremacy and particular laws by the external aid of God; witness only the two following passages:

(40) In Genesis xiv:18, 19, 20, it is related that Melchisedek was king of Jerusalem and priest of the Most High God, that in exercise of his priestly functions he blessed Abraham, and that Abraham the beloved of the Lord gave to this priest of God a tithe of all his spoils. (41) This sufficiently shows that before He founded the Israelitish nation God constituted kings and priests in Jerusalem, and ordained for them rites and laws. (42) Whether He did so prophetically is, as I have said, not sufficiently clear; but I am sure of this, that Abraham, whilst he sojourned in the city, lived scrupulously according to these laws, for Abraham had received no special rites from God; and yet it is stated (Gen. xxvi:5), that he observed the worship, the precepts, the statutes, and the laws of God, which must be interpreted to mean the worship, the statutes, the precepts, and the laws of king Melchisedek. (43) Malachi chides the Jews as follows (i:10-11.): "Who is there among you that will shut the doors? [of the Temple]; neither do ye kindle fire on mine altar for nought. (44) I have no pleasure in you, saith the Lord of Hosts. (45) For from the rising of the sun, even until the going down of the same My Name shall be great among the Gentiles; and in every place incense shall be offered in My Name, and a pure offering; for My Name is great among the heathen, saith the Lord of Hosts." (46) These words, which, unless we do violence to them, could only refer to the current period, abundantly testify that the Jews of that time were not more beloved by God than other nations, that God then favoured other nations with more miracles than He vouchsafed to the Jews, who had then partly recovered their empire without miraculous aid; and, lastly, that the Gentiles possessed rites and ceremonies acceptable to God. (47) But I pass over these points lightly: it is enough for my purpose to have shown that the election of the Jews had regard to nothing but temporal physical happiness and freedom, in other words, autonomous government, and to the manner and means by which they obtained it; consequently to the laws in so far as they were necessary to the preservation of that special government; and, lastly, to the manner in which they were revealed. In regard to other matters, wherein man's true happiness consists, they were on a par with the rest of the nations.

(48) When, therefore, it is said in Scripture (Deut. iv:7) that the Lord is not so nigh to any other nation as He is to the Jews, reference is only made to their government, and to the period when so many miracles happened to them, for in respect of intellect and virtue - that is, in respect of blessedness - God was, as we have said already, and are now demonstrating, equally gracious to all. (49) Scripture itself bears testimony to this fact, for the Psalmist says (cxlv:18), "The Lord is near unto all them that call upon Him, to all that call upon Him in truth." (50) So in the same Psalm, verse 9, "The Lord is good to all, and His tender mercies are over all His works." In Ps. xxxiii:16, it is clearly stated that God has granted to all men the same intellect, in these words, He fashioneth their hearts alike." The heart was considered by the Hebrews, as I suppose everyone knows, to be the seat of the soul and the intellect.

(51) Lastly, from Job xxxviii:28, it is plain that God had ordained for the whole human race the

law to reverence God, to keep from evil doing, or to do well, and that Job, although a Gentile, was of all men most acceptable to God, because he exceeded all in piety and religion. (52) Lastly, from Jonah iv:2, it is very evident that, not only to the Jews but to all men, God was gracious, merciful, long- suffering, and of great goodness, and repented Him of the evil, for Jonah says: "Therefore I determined to flee before unto Tarshish, for I know that Thou art a gracious God, and merciful, slow to anger, and of great kindness," &c., and that, therefore, God would pardon the Ninevites. (53) We conclude, therefore (inasmuch as God is to all men equally gracious, and the Hebrews were only, chosen by him in respect to their social organization and government), that the individual Jew, taken apart from his social organization and government, possessed no gift of God above other men, and that there was no difference between Jew and Gentile. (54) As it is a fact that God is equally gracious, merciful, and the rest, to all men; and as the function of the prophet was to teach men not so much the laws of their country, as true virtue, and to exhort them thereto, it is not to be doubted that all nations possessed prophets, and that the prophetic gift was not peculiar to the Jews. (55) Indeed, history, both profane and sacred, bears witness to the fact. (56) Although, from the sacred histories of the Old Testament, it is not evident that the other nations had as many prophets as the Hebrews, or that any Gentile prophet was expressly sent by God to the nations, this does not affect the question, for the Hebrews were careful to record their own affairs, not those of other nations. (57) It suffices, then, that we find in the Old Testament Gentiles, and uncircumcised, as Noah, Enoch, Abimelech, Balaam, &c., exercising prophetic gifts; further, that Hebrew prophets were sent by God, not only to their own nation but to many others also. (58) Ezekiel prophesied to all the nations then known; Obadiah to none, that we are aware of, save the Idumeans; and Jonah was chiefly the prophet to the Ninevites. (59) Isaiah bewails and predicts the calamities, and hails the restoration not only of the Jews but also of other nations, for he says (chap. xvi:9), "Therefore I will bewail Jazer with weeping;" and in chap. xix. he foretells first the calamities and then the restoration of the Egyptians (see verses 19, 20, 21, 25), saying that God shall send them a Saviour to free them, that the Lord shall be known in Egypt, and, further, that the Egyptians shall worship God with sacrifice and oblation; and, at last, he calls that nation the blessed Egyptian people of God; all of which particulars are specially noteworthy.

(60) Jeremiah is called, not the prophet of the Hebrew nation, but simply the prophet of the nations (see Jer:i.5). (61) He also mournfully foretells the calamities of the nations, and predicts their restoration, for he says (xlviii:31) of the Moabites, "Therefore will I howl for Moab, and I will cry out for all Moab" (verse 36), "and therefore mine heart shall sound for Moab like pipes;" in the end he prophesies their restoration, as also the restoration of the Egyptians, Ammonites, and Elamites. (62) Wherefore it is beyond doubt that other nations also, like the Jews, had their prophets, who prophesied to them.

(63) Although Scripture only, makes mention of one man, Balaam, to whom the future of the Jews and the other nations was revealed, we must not suppose that Balaam prophesied only once, for from the narrative itself it is abundantly clear that he had long previously been famous for prophesy and other Divine gifts. (64) For when Balak bade him to come to him, he said (Num.

xxii:6), "For I know that he whom thou blessest is blessed, and he whom thou cursest is cursed." (65) Thus we see that he possessed the gift which God had bestowed on Abraham. Further, as accustomed to prophesy, Balaam bade the messengers wait for him till the will of the Lord was revealed to him. (66) When he prophesied, that is, when he interpreted the true mind of God, he was wont to say this of himself: "He hath said, which heard the words of God and knew the knowledge of the Most High, which saw the vision of the Almighty falling into a trance, but having his eyes open." (67) Further, after he had blessed the Hebrews by the command of God, he began (as was his custom) to prophesy to other nations, and to predict their future; all of which abundantly shows that he had always been a prophet, or had often prophesied, and (as we may also remark here) possessed that which afforded the chief certainty to prophets of the truth of their prophecy, namely, a mind turned wholly to what is right and good, for he did not bless those whom he wished to bless, nor curse those whom he wished to curse, as Balak supposed, but only those whom God wished to be blessed or cursed. (68) Thus he answered Balak: "If Balak should give me his house full of silver and gold, I cannot go beyond the commandment of the Lord to do either good or bad of my own mind; but what the Lord saith, that will I speak." (69) As for God being angry with him in the way, the same happened to Moses when he set out to Egypt by the command of the Lord; and as to his receiving money for prophesying, Samuel did the same (1 Sam. ix:7, 8); if in anyway he sinned, "there is not a just man upon earth that doeth good and sinneth not," Eccles. vii:20. (Vide 2 Epist. Peter ii:15, 16, and Jude 5:11.)

(70) His speeches must certainly have had much weight with God, and His power for cursing must assuredly have been very great from the number of times that we find stated in Scripture, in proof of God's great mercy to the Jews, that God would not hear Balaam, and that He changed the cursing to blessing (see Deut. xxiii:6, Josh. xxiv:10, Neh. xiii:2). (71) Wherefore he was without doubt most acceptable to God, for the speeches and cursings of the wicked move God not at all. (72) As then he was a true prophet, and nevertheless Joshua calls him a soothsayer or augur, it is certain that this title had an honourable signification, and that those whom the Gentiles called augurs and soothsayers were true prophets, while those whom Scripture often accuses and condemns were false soothsayers, who deceived the Gentiles as false prophets deceived the Jews; indeed, this is made evident from other passages in the Bible, whence we conclude that the gift of prophecy was not peculiar to the Jews, but common to all nations. (73) The Pharisees, however, vehemently contend that this Divine gift was peculiar to their nation, and that the other nations foretold the future (what will superstition invent next?) by some unexplained diabolical faculty. (74) The principal passage of Scripture which they cite, by way of confirming their theory with its authority, is Exodus xxxiii:16, where Moses says to God, "For wherein shall it be known here that I and Thy people have found grace in Thy sight? is it not in that Thou goest with us? so shall we be separated, I and Thy people, from all the people that are upon the face of the earth." (75) From this they would infer that Moses asked of God that He should be present to the Jews, and should reveal Himself to them prophetically; further, that He should grant this favour to no other nation. (76) It is surely absurd that Moses should have been jealous of God's presence among the Gentiles, or that he should have dared to ask any such thing.

(77) The act is, as Moses knew that the disposition and spirit of his nation was rebellious, he clearly saw that they could not carry out what they had begun without very great miracles and special external aid from God; nay, that without such aid they must necessarily perish: as it was evident that God wished them to be preserved, he asked for this special external aid. (78) Thus he says (Ex. xxxiv:9), "If now I have found grace in Thy sight, 0 Lord, let my Lord, I pray Thee, go among us; for it is a stiffnecked people." (79) The reason, therefore, for his seeking special external aid from God was the stiffneckedness of the people, and it is made still more plain, that he asked for nothing beyond this special external aid by God's answer - for God answered at once (verse 10 of the same chapter) - "Behold, I make a covenant: before all Thy people I will do marvels, such as have not been done in all the earth, nor in any nation." (80) Therefore Moses had in view nothing beyond the special election of the Jews, as I have explained it, and made no other request to God. (81) I confess that in Paul's Epistle to the Romans, I find another text which carries more weight, namely, where Paul seems to teach a different doctrine from that here set down, for he there says (Rom. iii:1): "What advantage then hath the Jew? or what profit is there of circumcision? (82) Much every way: chiefly, because that unto them were committed the oracles of God."

(83) But if we look to the doctrine which Paul especially desired to teach, we shall find nothing repugnant to our present contention; on the contrary, his doctrine is the same as ours, for he says (Rom. iii:29) "that God is the God of the Jews and of the Gentiles, and" (ch. ii:25, 26) "But, if thou be a breaker of the law, thy circumcision is made uncircumcision. (84) Therefore if the uncircumcision keep the righteousness of the law, shall not his uncircumcision be counted for circumcision?" (85) Further, in chap. iv:verse 9, he says that all alike, Jew and Gentile, were under sin, and that without commandment and law there is no sin. (86) Wherefore it is most evident that to all men absolutely was revealed the law under which all lived - namely, the law which has regard only to true virtue, not the law established in respect to, and in the formation of a particular state and adapted to the disposition of a particular people. (87) Lastly, Paul concludes that since God is the God of all nations, that is, is equally gracious to all, and since all men equally live under the law and under sin, so also to all nations did God send His Christ, to free all men equally from the bondage of the law, that they should no more do right by the command of the law, but by the constant determination of their hearts. (88) So that Paul teaches exactly the same as ourselves. (89) When, therefore, he says "To the Jews only were entrusted the oracles of God," we must either understand that to them only were the laws entrusted in writing, while they were given to other nations merely in revelation and conception, or else (as none but Jews would object to the doctrine he desired to advance) that Paul was answering only in accordance with the understanding and current ideas of the Jews, for in respect to teaching things which he had partly seen, partly heard, he was to the Greeks a Greek, and to the Jews a Jew.

(90) It now only remains to us to answer the arguments of those who would persuade themselves that the election of the Jews was not temporal, and merely in respect of their commonwealth, but eternal; for, they say, we see the Jews after the loss of their commonwealth,

and after being scattered so many years and separated from all other nations, still surviving, which is without parallel among other peoples, and further the Scriptures seem to teach that God has chosen for Himself the Jews for ever, so that though they have lost their commonwealth, they still nevertheless remain God's elect.

(91) The passages which they think teach most clearly this eternal election, are chiefly: (1.) Jer. xxxi:36, where the prophet testifies that the seed of Israel shall for ever remain the nation of God, comparing them with the stability of the heavens and nature;

(2.) Ezek. xx:32, where the prophet seems to intend that though the Jews wanted after the help afforded them to turn their backs on the worship of the Lord, that God would nevertheless gather them together again from all the lands in which they were dispersed, and lead them to the wilderness of the peoples - as He had led their fathers to the wilderness of the land of Egypt - and would at length, after purging out from among them the rebels and transgressors, bring them thence to his Holy mountain, where the whole house of Israel should worship Him. Other passages are also cited, especially by the Pharisees, but I think I shall satisfy everyone if I answer these two, and this I shall easily accomplish after showing from Scripture itself that God chose not the Hebrews for ever, but only on the condition under which He had formerly chosen the Canaanites, for these last, as we have shown, had priests who religiously worshipped God, and whom God at length rejected because of their luxury, pride, and corrupt worship.

(92) Moses (Lev. xviii:27) warned the Israelites that they be not polluted with whoredoms, lest the land spue them out as it had spued out the nations who had dwelt there before, and in Deut. viii:19, 20, in the plainest terms He threatens their total ruin, for He says, "I testify against you that ye shall surely perish. (93) As the nations which the Lord destroyeth before your face, so shall ye perish." In like manner many other passages are found in the law which expressly show that God chose the Hebrews neither absolutely nor for ever. (94) If, then, the prophets foretold for them a new covenant of the knowledge of God, love, and grace, such a promise is easily proved to be only made to the elect, for Ezekiel in the chapter which we have just quoted expressly says that God will separate from them the rebellious and transgressors, and Zephaniah (iii:12, 13), says that "God will take away the proud from the midst of them, and leave the poor." (95) Now, inasmuch as their election has regard to true virtue, it is not to be thought that it was promised to the Jews alone to the exclusion of others, but we must evidently believe that the true Gentile prophets (and every nation, as we have shown, possessed such) promised the same to the faithful of their own people, who were thereby comforted. (96) Wherefore this eternal covenant of the knowledge of God and love is universal, as is clear, moreover, from Zeph. iii:10, 11: no difference in this respect can be admitted between Jew and Gentile, nor did the former enjoy any special election beyond that which we have pointed out.

(97) When the prophets, in speaking of this election which regards only true virtue, mixed up much concerning sacrifices and ceremonies, and the rebuilding of the temple and city, they wished by such figurative expressions, after the manner and nature of prophecy, to expound matters spiritual, so as at the same time to show to the Jews, whose prophets they were, the true restoration of the state and of the temple to be expected about the time of Cyrus.

(98) At the present time, therefore, there is absolutely nothing which the Jews can arrogate to themselves beyond other people.

(99) As to their continuance so long after dispersion and the loss of empire, there is nothing marvellous in it, for they so separated themselves from every other nation as to draw down upon themselves universal hate, not only by their outward rites, rites conflicting with those of other nations, but also by the sign of circumcision which they most scrupulously observe.

(100) That they have been preserved in great measure by Gentile hatred, experience demonstrates. (101) When the king of Spain formerly compelled the Jews to embrace the State religion or to go into exile, a large number of Jews accepted Catholicism. (102) Now, as these renegades were admitted to all the native privileges of Spaniards, and deemed worthy of filling all honourable offices, it came to pass that they straightway became so intermingled with the Spaniards as to leave of themselves no relic or remembrance. (103) But exactly the opposite happened to those whom the king of Portugal compelled to become Christians, for they always, though converted, lived apart, inasmuch as they were considered unworthy of any civic honours.

(104) The sign of circumcision is, as I think, so important, that I could persuade myself that it alone would preserve the nation for ever. (105) Nay, I would go so far as to believe that if the foundations of their religion have not emasculated their minds they may even, if occasion offers, so changeable are human affairs, raise up their empire afresh, and that God may a second time elect them.

(106) Of such a possibility we have a very famous example in the Chinese. (107) They, too, have some distinctive mark on their heads which they most scrupulously observe, and by which they keep themselves apart from everyone else, and have thus kept themselves during so many thousand years that they far surpass all other nations in antiquity. (108) They have not always retained empire, but they have recovered it when lost, and doubtless will do so again after the spirit of the Tartars becomes relaxed through the luxury of riches and pride.

(109) Lastly, if any one wishes to maintain that the Jews, from this or from any other cause, have been chosen by God for ever, I will not gainsay him if he will admit that this choice, whether temporary or eternal, has no regard, in so far as it is peculiar to the Jews, to aught but dominion and physical advantages (for by such alone can one nation be distinguished from another), whereas in regard to intellect and true virtue, every nation is on a par with the rest, and God has not in these respects chosen one people rather than another.

CHAPTER IV. - OF THE DIVINE LAW.

(1) The word law, taken in the abstract, means that by which an individual, or all things, or as many things as belong to a particular species, act in one and the same fixed and definite manner, which manner depends either on natural necessity or on human decree. (2) A law which depends on natural necessity is one which necessarily follows from the nature, or from the definition of the thing in question; a law which depends on human decree, and which is more correctly called an ordinance, is one which men have laid down for themselves and others in order to live more safely or conveniently, or from some similar reason.

(3) For example, the law that all bodies impinging on lesser bodies, lose as much of their own motion as they communicate to the latter is a universal law of all bodies, and depends on natural necessity. (4) So, too, the law that a man in remembering one thing, straightway remembers another either like it, or which he had perceived simultaneously with it, is a law which necessarily follows from the nature of man. (5) But the law that men must yield, or be compelled to yield, somewhat of their natural right, and that they bind themselves to live in a certain way, depends on human decree. (6) Now, though I freely admit that all things are predetermined by universal natural laws to exist and operate in a given, fixed, and definite manner, I still assert that the laws I have just mentioned depend on human decree.

(1.) (7) Because man, in so far as he is a part of nature, constitutes a part of the power of nature. (8) Whatever, therefore, follows necessarily from the necessity of human nature (that is, from nature herself, in so far as we conceive of her as acting through man) follows, even though it be necessarily, from human power. (9) Hence the sanction of such laws may very well be said to depend on man's decree, for it principally depends on the power of the human mind; so that the human mind in respect to its perception of things as true and false, can readily be conceived as without such laws, but not without necessary law as we have just defined it.

(2.) (10) I have stated that these laws depend on human decree because it is well to define and explain things by their proximate causes. (11) The general consideration of fate and the concatenation of causes would aid us very little in forming and arranging our ideas concerning particular questions. (12) Let us add that as to the actual coordination and concatenation of things, that is how things are ordained and linked together, we are obviously ignorant; therefore, it is more profitable for right living, nay, it is necessary for us to consider things as contingent. (13) So much about law in the abstract.

(14) Now the word law seems to be only applied to natural phenomena by analogy, and is commonly taken to signify a command which men can either obey or neglect, inasmuch as it restrains human nature within certain originally exceeded limits, and therefore lays down no rule beyond human strength. (15) Thus it is expedient to define law more particularly as a plan of life laid down by man for himself or others with a certain object.

(16) However, as the true object of legislation is only perceived by a few, and most men are almost incapable of grasping it, though they live under its conditions, legislators, with a view to exacting general obedience, have wisely put forward another object, very different from that

which necessarily follows from the nature of law: they promise to the observers of the law that which the masses chiefly desire, and threaten its violators with that which they chiefly fear: thus endeavouring to restrain the masses, as far as may be, like a horse with a curb; whence it follows that the word law is chiefly applied to the modes of life enjoined on men by the sway of others; hence those who obey the law are said to live under it and to be under compulsion. (17) In truth, a man who renders everyone their due because he fears the gallows, acts under the sway and compulsion of others, and cannot be called just. (18) But a man who does the same from a knowledge of the true reason for laws and their necessity, acts from a firm purpose and of his own accord, and is therefore properly called just. (19) This, I take it, is Paul's meaning when he says, that those who live under the law cannot be justified through the law, for justice, as commonly defined, is the constant and perpetual will to render every man his due. (20) Thus Solomon says (Prov. xxi:15), "It is a joy to the just to do judgment," but the wicked fear.

(21) Law, then, being a plan of living which men have for a certain object laid down for themselves or others, may, as it seems, be divided into human law and Divine law. {But both are opposite sides of the same coin}

(22) By human law I mean a plan of living which serves only to render life and the state secure. (23) By Divine law I mean that which only regards the highest good, in other words, the true knowledge of God and love.

(24) I call this law Divine because of the nature of the highest good, which I will here shortly explain as clearly as I can.

(25) Inasmuch as the intellect is the best part of our being, it is evident that we should make every effort to perfect it as far as possible if we desire to search for what is really profitable to us. (26) For in intellectual perfection the highest good should consist. (27) Now, since all our knowledge, and the certainty which removes every doubt, depend solely on the knowledge of God;- firstly, because without God nothing can exist or be conceived; secondly, because so long as we have no clear and distinct idea of God we may remain in universal doubt - it follows that our highest good and perfection also depend solely on the knowledge of God. (28) Further, since without God nothing can exist or be conceived, it is evident that all natural phenomena involve and express the conception of God as far as their essence and perfection extend, so that we have greater and more perfect knowledge of God in proportion to our knowledge of natural phenomena: conversely (since the knowledge of an effect through its cause is the same thing as the knowledge of a particular property of a cause) the greater our knowledge of natural phenomena, the more perfect is our knowledge of the essence of God (which is the cause of all things). (29) So, then, our highest good not only depends on the knowledge of God, but wholly consists therein; and it further follows that man is perfect or the reverse in proportion to the nature and perfection of the object of his special desire; hence the most perfect and the chief sharer in the highest blessedness is he who prizes above all else, and takes especial delight in, the intellectual knowledge of God, the most perfect Being.

(30) Hither, then, our highest good and our highest blessedness aim - namely, to the knowledge and love of God; therefore the means demanded by this aim of all human actions, that is, by God

in so far as the idea of him is in us, may be called the commands of God, because they proceed, as it were, from God Himself, inasmuch as He exists in our minds, and the plan of life which has regard to this aim may be fitly called the law of God.

(31) The nature of the means, and the plan of life which this aim demands, how the foundations of the best states follow its lines, and how men's life is conducted, are questions pertaining to general ethics. (32) Here I only proceed to treat of the Divine law in a particular application.

(33) As the love of God is man's highest happiness and blessedness, and the ultimate end and aim of all human actions, it follows that he alone lives by the Divine law who loves God not from fear of punishment, or from love of any other object, such as sensual pleasure, fame, or the like; but solely because he has knowledge of God, or is convinced that the knowledge and love of God is the highest good. (34) The sum and chief precept, then, of the Divine law is to love God as the highest good, namely, as we have said, not from fear of any pains and penalties, or from the love of any other object in which we desire to take pleasure. (35) The idea of God lays down the rule that God is our highest good - in other words, that the knowledge and love of God is the ultimate aim to which all our actions should be directed. (36) The worldling cannot understand these things, they appear foolishness to him, because he has too meager a knowledge of God, and also because in this highest good he can discover nothing which he can handle or eat, or which affects the fleshly appetites wherein he chiefly delights, for it consists solely in thought and the pure reason. (37) They, on the other hand, who know that they possess no greater gift than intellect and sound reason, will doubtless accept what I have said without question.

(38) We have now explained that wherein the Divine law chiefly consists, and what are human laws, namely, all those which have a different aim unless they have been ratified by revelation, for in this respect also things are referred to God (as we have shown above) and in this sense the law of Moses, although it was not universal, but entirely adapted to the disposition and particular preservation of a single people, may yet be called a law of God or Divine law, inasmuch as we believe that it was ratified by prophetic insight. (39) If we consider the nature of natural Divine law as we have just explained it, we shall see:

(40) I.- That it is universal or common to all men, for we have deduced it from universal human nature.

(41) II. That it does not depend on the truth of any historical narrative whatsoever, for inasmuch as this natural Divine law is comprehended solely by the consideration of human nature, it is plain that we can conceive it as existing as well in Adam as in any other man, as well in a man living among his fellows, as in a man who lives by himself.

(42) The truth of a historical narrative, however assured, cannot give us the knowledge nor consequently the love of God, for love of God springs from knowledge of Him, and knowledge of Him should be derived from general ideas, in themselves certain and known, so that the truth of a historical narrative is very far from being a necessary requisite for our attaining our highest good.

(43) Still, though the truth of histories cannot give us the knowledge and love of God, I do not deny that reading them is very useful with a view to life in the world, for the more we have

observed and known of men's customs and circumstances, which are best revealed by their actions, the more warily we shall be able to order our lives among them, and so far as reason dictates to adapt our actions to their dispositions.

(44) III. We see that this natural Divine law does not demand the performance of ceremonies - that is, actions in themselves indifferent, which are called good from the fact of their institution, or actions symbolizing something profitable for salvation, or (if one prefers this definition) actions of which the meaning surpasses human understanding. (45) The natural light of reason does not demand anything which it is itself unable to supply, but only such as it can very clearly show to be good, or a means to our blessedness. (46) Such things as are good simply because they have been commanded or instituted, or as being symbols of something good, are mere shadows which cannot be reckoned among actions that are the offsprings as it were, or fruit of a sound mind and of intellect. (47) There is no need for me to go into this now in more detail.

(48) IV. Lastly, we see that the highest reward of the Divine law is the law itself, namely, to know God and to love Him of our free choice, and with an undivided and fruitful spirit; while its penalty is the absence of these things, and being in bondage to the flesh - that is, having an inconstant and wavering spirit.

(49) These points being noted, I must now inquire:

(50) I. Whether by the natural light of reason we can conceive of God as a law-giver or potentate ordaining laws for men?

(51) II. What is the teaching of Holy Writ concerning this natural light of reason and natural law?

(52) III. With what objects were ceremonies formerly instituted?

(53) IV. Lastly, what is the good gained by knowing the sacred histories and believing them?

(54) Of the first two I will treat in this chapter, of the remaining two in the following one.

(55) Our conclusion about the first is easily deduced from the nature of God's will, which is only distinguished from His understanding in relation to our intellect - that is, the will and the understanding of God are in reality one and the same, and are only distinguished in relation to our thoughts which we form concerning God's understanding. (56) For instance, if we are only looking to the fact that the nature of a triangle is from eternity contained in the Divine nature as an eternal verity, we say that God possesses the idea of a triangle, or that He understands the nature of a triangle; but if afterwards we look to the fact that the nature of a triangle is thus contained in the Divine nature, solely by the necessity of the Divine nature, and not by the necessity of the nature and essence of a triangle - in fact, that the necessity of a triangle's essence and nature, in so far as they are conceived of as eternal verities, depends solely on the necessity of the Divine nature and intellect, we then style God's will or decree, that which before we styled His intellect. (57) Wherefore we make one and the same affirmation concerning God when we say that He has from eternity decreed that three angles of a triangle are equal to two right angles, as when we say that He has understood it.

(58) Hence the affirmations and the negations of God always involve necessity or truth; so that, for example, if God said to Adam that He did not wish him to eat of the tree of knowledge of

good and evil, it would have involved a contradiction that Adam should have been able to eat of it, and would therefore have been impossible that he should have so eaten, for the Divine command would have involved an eternal necessity and truth. (59) But since Scripture nevertheless narrates that God did give this command to Adam, and yet that none the less Adam ate of the tree, we must perforce say that God revealed to Adam the evil which would surely follow if he should eat of the tree, but did not disclose that such evil would of necessity come to pass. (60) Thus it was that Adam took the revelation to be not an eternal and necessary truth, but a law - that is, an ordinance followed by gain or loss, not depending necessarily on the nature of the act performed, but solely on the will and absolute power of some potentate, so that the revelation in question was solely in relation to Adam, and solely through his lack of knowledge a law, and God was, as it were, a lawgiver and potentate. (61) From the same cause, namely, from lack of knowledge, the Decalogue in relation to the Hebrews was a law, for since they knew not the existence of God as an eternal truth, they must have taken as a law that which was revealed to them in the Decalogue, namely, that God exists, and that God only should be worshipped. (62) But if God had spoken to them without the intervention of any bodily means, immediately they would have perceived it not as a law, but as an eternal truth.

(63) What we have said about the Israelites and Adam, applies also to all the prophets who wrote laws in God's name - they did not adequately conceive God's decrees as eternal truths. (64) For instance, we must say of Moses that from revelation, from the basis of what was revealed to him, he perceived the method by which the Israelitish nation could best be united in a particular territory, and could form a body politic or state, and further that he perceived the method by which that nation could best be constrained to obedience; but he did not perceive, nor was it revealed to him, that this method was absolutely the best, nor that the obedience of the people in a certain strip of territory would necessarily imply the end he had in view. (65) Wherefore he perceived these things not as eternal truths, but as precepts and ordinances, and he ordained them as laws of God, and thus it came to be that he conceived God as a ruler, a legislator, a king, as merciful, just, &c., whereas such qualities are simply attributes of human nature, and utterly alien from the nature of the Deity. (66) Thus much we may affirm of the prophets who wrote laws in the name of God; but we must not affirm it of Christ, for Christ, although He too seems to have written laws in the name of God, must be taken to have had a clear and adequate perception, for Christ was not so much a prophet as the mouthpiece of God. (67) For God made revelations to mankind through Christ as He had before done through angels - that is, a created voice, visions, &c. (68) It would be as unreasonable to say that God had accommodated his revelations to the opinions of Christ as that He had before accommodated them to the opinions of angels (that is, of a created voice or visions) as matters to be revealed to the prophets, a wholly absurd hypothesis. (69) Moreover, Christ was sent to teach not only the Jews but the whole human race, and therefore it was not enough that His mind should be accommodated to the opinions the Jews alone, but also to the opinion and fundamental teaching common to the whole human race - in other words, to ideas universal and true. (70) Inasmuch as God revealed Himself to Christ, or to Christ's mind immediately, and not as to the prophets through words and symbols,

we must needs suppose that Christ perceived truly what was revealed, in other words, He understood it, for a matter is understood when it is perceived simply by the mind without words or symbols.

(71) Christ, then, perceived (truly and adequately) what was revealed, and if He ever proclaimed such revelations as laws, He did so because of the ignorance and obstinacy of the people, acting in this respect the part of God; inasmuch as He accommodated Himself to the comprehension of the people, and though He spoke somewhat more clearly than the other prophets, yet He taught what was revealed obscurely, and generally through parables, especially when He was speaking to those to whom it was not yet given to understand the kingdom of heaven. (See Matt. xiii:10, &c.) (72) To those to whom it was given to understand the mysteries of heaven, He doubtless taught His doctrines as eternal truths, and did not lay them down as laws, thus freeing the minds of His hearers from the bondage of that law which He further confirmed and established. (73) Paul apparently points to this more than once (e.g. Rom. vii:6, and iii:28), though he never himself seems to wish to speak openly, but, to quote his own words (Rom. iii:6, and vi:19), "merely humanly." (74) This he expressly states when he calls God just, and it was doubtless in concession to human weakness that he attributes mercy, grace, anger, and similar qualities to God, adapting his language to the popular mind, or, as he puts it (1 Cor. iii:1, 2), to carnal men. (75) In Rom. ix:18, he teaches undisguisedly that God's auger and mercy depend not on the actions of men, but on God's own nature or will; further, that no one is justified by the works of the law, but only by faith, which he seems to identify with the full assent of the soul; lastly, that no one is blessed unless he have in him the mind of Christ (Rom. viii:9), whereby he perceives the laws of God as eternal truths. (76) We conclude, therefore, that God is described as a lawgiver or prince, and styled just, merciful, &c., merely in concession to popular understanding, and the imperfection of popular knowledge; that in reality God acts and directs all things simply by the necessity of His nature and perfection, and that His decrees and volitions are eternal truths, and always involve necessity. (77) So much for the first point which I wished to explain and demonstrate.

(78) Passing on to the second point, let us search the sacred pages for their teaching concerning the light of nature and this Divine law. (79) The first doctrine we find in the history of the first man, where it is narrated that God commanded Adam not to eat of the fruit of the tree of the knowledge of good and evil; this seems to mean that God commanded Adam to do and to seek after righteousness because it was good, not because the contrary was evil: that is, to seek the good for its own sake, not from fear of evil. (80) We have seen that he who acts rightly from the true knowledge and love of right, acts with freedom and constancy, whereas he who acts from fear of evil, is under the constraint of evil, and acts in bondage under external control. (81) So that this commandment of God to Adam comprehends the whole Divine natural law, and absolutely agrees with the dictates of the light of nature; nay, it would be easy to explain on this basis the whole history or allegory of the first man. (82) But I prefer to pass over the subject in silence, because, in the first place, I cannot be absolutely certain that my explanation would be in accordance with the intention of the sacred writer; and, secondly, because many do not admit

that this history is an allegory, maintaining it to be a simple narrative of facts. (83) It will be better, therefore, to adduce other passages of Scripture, especially such as were written by him, who speaks with all the strength of his natural understanding, in which he surpassed all his contemporaries, and whose sayings are accepted by the people as of equal weight with those of the prophets. (84) I mean Solomon, whose prudence and wisdom are commended in Scripture rather than his piety and gift of prophecy. (85) Life being taken to mean the true life (as is evident from Deut. xxx:19), the fruit of the understanding consists only in the true life, and its absence constitutes punishment. (86) All this absolutely agrees with what was set out in our fourth point concerning natural law. (87) Moreover our position that it is the well-spring of life, and that the intellect alone lays down laws for the wise, is plainly taught by, the sage, for he says (Prov. xiii:14): "The law of the wise is a fountain of life" - that is, as we gather from the preceding text, the understanding. (88) In chap. iii:13, he expressly teaches that the understanding renders man blessed and happy, and gives him true peace of mind. "Happy is the man that findeth wisdom, and the man that getteth understanding," for "Wisdom gives length of days, and riches and honour; her ways are ways of pleasantness, and all her paths peace" (xiiii:6, 17). (89) According to Solomon, therefore, it is only, the wise who live in peace and equanimity, not like the wicked whose minds drift hither and thither, and (as Isaiah says, chap. lvii:20) "are like the troubled sea, for them there is no peace."

(90) Lastly, we should especially note the passage in chap. ii. of Solomon's proverbs which most clearly confirms our contention: "If thou criest after knowledge, and liftest up thy voice for understanding . . . then shalt thou understand the fear of the Lord, and find the knowledge of God; for the Lord giveth wisdom; out of His mouth cometh knowledge and understanding." (91) These words clearly enunciate (1), that wisdom or intellect alone teaches us to fear God wisely - that is, to worship Him truly; (2), that wisdom and knowledge flow from God's mouth, and that God bestows on us this gift; this we have already shown in proving that our understanding and our knowledge depend on, spring from, and are perfected by the idea or knowledge of God, and nothing else. (92) Solomon goes on to say in so many words that this knowledge contains and involves the true principles of ethics and politics: "When wisdom entereth into thy heart, and knowledge is pleasant to thy soul, discretion shall preserve thee, understanding shall keep thee, then shalt thou understand righteousness, and judgment, and equity, yea every good path." (93) All of which is in obvious agreement with natural knowledge: for after we have come to the understanding of things, and have tasted the excellence of knowledge, she teaches us ethics and true virtue.

(94) Thus the happiness and the peace of him who cultivates his natural understanding lies, according to Solomon also, not so much under the dominion of fortune (or God's external aid) as in inward personal virtue (or God's internal aid), for the latter can to a great extent be preserved by vigilance, right action, and thought.

(95) Lastly, we must by no means pass over the passage in Paul's Epistle to the Romans, i:20, in which he says: "For the invisible things of God from the creation of the world are clearly seen, being understood by the things that are made, even His eternal power and Godhead; so that they

are without excuse, because, when they knew God, they glorified Him not as God, neither were they thankful." (96) These words clearly show that everyone can by the light of nature clearly understand the goodness and the eternal divinity of God, and can thence know and deduce what they should seek for and what avoid; wherefore the Apostle says that they are without excuse and cannot plead ignorance, as they certainly might if it were a question of supernatural light and the incarnation, passion, and resurrection of Christ. (97) "Wherefore," he goes on to say (ib. 24), "God gave them up to uncleanness through the lusts of their own hearts;" and so on, through the rest of the chapter, he describes the vices of ignorance, and sets them forth as the punishment of ignorance. (98) This obviously agrees with the verse of Solomon, already quoted, "The instruction of fools is folly," so that it is easy to understand why Paul says that the wicked are without excuse. (99) As every man sows so shall he reap: out of evil, evils necessarily spring, unless they be wisely counteracted.

(100) Thus we see that Scripture literally approves of the light of natural reason and the natural Divine law, and I have fulfilled the promises made at the beginning of this chapter.

CHAPTER V. - OF THE CEREMONIAL LAW.

(1) In the foregoing chapter we have shown that the Divine law, which renders men truly blessed, and teaches them the true life, is universal to all men; nay, we have so intimately deduced it from human nature that it must be esteemed innate, and, as it were, ingrained in the human mind.

(2) But with regard to the ceremonial observances which were ordained in the Old Testament for the Hebrews only, and were so adapted to their state that they could for the most part only be observed by the society as a whole and not by each individual, it is evident that they formed no part of the Divine law, and had nothing to do with blessedness and virtue, but had reference only to the election of the Hebrews, that is (as I have shown in Chap. II.), to their temporal bodily happiness and the tranquillity of their kingdom, and that therefore they were only valid while that kingdom lasted. (3) If in the Old Testament they are spoken of as the law of God, it is only because they were founded on revelation, or a basis of revelation. (4) Still as reason, however sound, has little weight with ordinary theologians, I will adduce the authority of Scripture for what I here assert, and will further show, for the sake of greater clearness, why and how these ceremonials served to establish and preserve the Jewish kingdom. (5) Isaiah teaches most plainly that the Divine law in its strict sense signifies that universal law which consists in a true manner of life, and does not signify ceremonial observances. (6) In chapter i:10, the prophet calls on his countrymen to hearken to the Divine law as he delivers it, and first excluding all kinds of sacrifices and all feasts, he at length sums up the law in these few words, "Cease to do evil, learn to do well: seek judgment, relieve the oppressed." (7) Not less striking testimony is given in Psalm xl:7- 9, where the Psalmist addresses God: "Sacrifice and offering Thou didst not desire; mine ears hast Thou opened; burnt offering and sin-offering hast Thou not required; I delight to do Thy will, 0 my God; yea, Thy law is within my heart." (8) Here the Psalmist reckons as the law of God only that which is inscribed in his heart, and excludes ceremonies therefrom, for the latter are good and inscribed on the heart only from the fact of their institution, and not because of their intrinsic value.

(9) Other passages of Scripture testify to the same truth, but these two will suffice. (10) We may also learn from the Bible that ceremonies are no aid to blessedness, but only have reference to the temporal prosperity of the kingdom; for the rewards promised for their observance are merely temporal advantages and delights, blessedness being reserved for the universal Divine law. (11) In all the five books commonly attributed to Moses nothing is promised, as I have said, beyond temporal benefits, such as honours, fame, victories, riches, enjoyments, and health. (12) Though many moral precepts besides ceremonies are contained in these five books, they appear not as moral doctrines universal to all men, but as commands especially adapted to the understanding and character of the Hebrew people, and as having reference only to the welfare of the kingdom. (13) For instance, Moses does not teach the Jews as a prophet not to kill or to steal, but gives these commandments solely as a lawgiver and judge; he does not reason out the doctrine, but affixes for its non-observance a penalty which may and very properly does vary in

different nations. (14) So, too, the command not to commit adultery is given merely with reference to the welfare of the state; for if the moral doctrine had been intended, with reference not only to the welfare of the state, but also to the tranquillity and blessedness of the individual, Moses would have condemned not merely the outward act, but also the mental acquiescence, as is done by Christ, Who taught only universal moral precepts, and for this cause promises a spiritual instead of a temporal reward. (15) Christ, as I have said, was sent into the world, not to preserve the state nor to lay down laws, but solely to teach the universal moral law, so we can easily understand that He wished in nowise to do away with the law of Moses, inasmuch as He introduced no new laws of His own - His sole care was to teach moral doctrines, and distinguish them from the laws of the state; for the Pharisees, in their ignorance, thought that the observance of the state law and the Mosaic law was the sum total of morality; whereas such laws merely had reference to the public welfare, and aimed not so much at instructing the Jews as at keeping them under constraint. (16) But let us return to our subject, and cite other passages of Scripture which set forth temporal benefits as rewards for observing the ceremonial law, and blessedness as reward for the universal law.

(17) None of the prophets puts the point more clearly than Isaiah. (18.) After condemning hypocrisy he commends liberty and charity towards one's self and one's neighbours, and promises as a reward: "Then shall thy light break forth as the morning, and thy health shall spring forth speedily, thy righteousness shall go before thee, and the glory of the Lord shall be thy reward" (chap. lviii:8). (19) Shortly afterwards he commends the Sabbath, and for a due observance of it, promises: "Then shalt thou delight thyself in the Lord, and I will cause thee to ride upon the high places of the earth, and feed thee with the heritage of Jacob thy father: for the mouth of the Lord has spoken it." (20) Thus the prophet for liberty bestowed, and charitable works, promises a healthy mind in a healthy body, and the glory of the Lord even after death; whereas, for ceremonial exactitude, he only promises security of rule, prosperity, and temporal happiness.

(21) In Psalms xv. and xxiv. no mention is made of ceremonies, but only of moral doctrines, inasmuch as there is no question of anything but blessedness, and blessedness is symbolically promised: it is quite certain that the expressions, "the hill of God," and "His tents and the dwellers therein," refer to blessedness and security of soul, not to the actual mount of Jerusalem and the tabernacle of Moses, for these latter were not dwelt in by anyone, and only the sons of Levi ministered there. (22) Further, all those sentences of Solomon to which I referred in the last chapter, for the cultivation of the intellect and wisdom, promise true blessedness, for by wisdom is the fear of God at length understood, and the knowledge of God found.

(23) That the Jews themselves were not bound to practise their ceremonial observances after the destruction of their kingdom is evident from Jeremiah. (24) For when the prophet saw and foretold that the desolation of the city was at hand, he said that God only delights in those who know and understand that He exercises loving-kindness, judgment, and righteousness in the earth, and that such persons only are worthy of praise. (Jer. ix:23.) (25) As though God had said that, after the desolation of the city, He would require nothing special from the Jews beyond the

natural law by which all men are bound.

(26) The New Testament also confirms this view, for only moral doctrines are therein taught, and the kingdom of heaven is promised as a reward, whereas ceremonial observances are not touched on by the Apostles, after they began to preach the Gospel to the Gentiles. (27) The Pharisees certainly continued to practise these rites after the destruction of the kingdom, but more with a view of opposing the Christians than of pleasing God: for after the first destruction of the city, when they were led captive to Babylon, not being then, so far as I am aware, split up into sects, they straightway neglected their rites, bid farewell to the Mosaic law, buried their national customs in oblivion as being plainly superfluous, and began to mingle with other nations, as we may abundantly learn from Ezra and Nehemiah. (28) We cannot, therefore, doubt that they were no more bound by the law of Moses, after the destruction of their kingdom, than they had been before it had been begun, while they were still living among other peoples before the exodus from Egypt, and were subject to no special law beyond the natural law, and also, doubtless, the law of the state in which they were living, in so far as it was consonant with the Divine natural law.

(29) As to the fact that the patriarchs offered sacrifices, I think they did so for the purpose of stimulating their piety, for their minds had been accustomed from childhood to the idea of sacrifice, which we know had been universal from the time of Enoch; and thus they found in sacrifice their most powerful incentive. (30) The patriarchs, then, did not sacrifice to God at the bidding of a Divine right, or as taught by the basis of the Divine law, but simply in accordance with the custom of the time; and, if in so doing they followed any ordinance, it was simply the ordinance of the country they were living in, by which (as we have seen before in the case of Melchisedek) they were bound.

(31) I think that I have now given Scriptural authority for my view: it remains to show why and how the ceremonial observances tended to preserve and confirm the Hebrew kingdom; and this I can very briefly do on grounds universally accepted.

(32) The formation of society serves not only for defensive purposes, but is also very useful, and, indeed, absolutely necessary, as rendering possible the division of labour. (33) If men did not render mutual assistance to each other, no one would have either the skill or the time to provide for his own sustenance and preservation: for all men are not equally apt for all work, and no one would be capable of preparing all that he individually stood in need of. (34) Strength and time, I repeat, would fail, if every one had in person to plough, to sow, to reap, to grind corn, to cook, to weave, to stitch, and perform the other numerous functions required to keep life going; to say nothing of the arts and sciences which are also entirely necessary to the perfection and blessedness of human nature. (35) We see that peoples living, in uncivilized barbarism lead a wretched and almost animal life, and even they would not be able to acquire their few rude necessaries without assisting one another to a certain extent.

(36) Now if men were so constituted by nature that they desired nothing but what is designated by true reason, society would obviously have no need of laws: it would be sufficient to inculcate true moral doctrines; and men would freely, without hesitation, act in accordance with their true

interests. (37) But human nature is framed in a different fashion: every one, indeed, seeks his own interest, but does not do so in accordance with the dictates of sound reason, for most men's ideas of desirability and usefulness are guided by their fleshly instincts and emotions, which take no thought beyond the present and the immediate object. (38) Therefore, no society can exist without government, and force, and laws to restrain and repress men's desires and immoderate impulses. (39) Still human nature will not submit to absolute repression. (40) Violent governments, as Seneca says, never last long; the moderate governments endure. (41) So long as men act simply from fear they act contrary to their inclinations, taking no thought for the advantages or necessity of their actions, but simply endeavouring to escape punishment or loss of life. (42) They must needs rejoice in any evil which befalls their ruler, even if it should involve themselves; and must long for and bring about such evil by every means in their power. (43) Again, men are especially intolerant of serving and being ruled by their equals. (44) Lastly, it is exceedingly difficult to revoke liberties once granted.

(45) From these considerations it follows, firstly, that authority should either be vested in the hands of the whole state in common, so that everyone should be bound to serve, and yet not be in subjection to his equals; or else, if power be in the hands of a few, or one man, that one man should be something above average humanity, or should strive to get himself accepted as such. (46) Secondly, laws should in every government be so arranged that people should be kept in bounds by the hope of some greatly desired good, rather than by fear, for then everyone will do his duty willingly.

(47) Lastly, as obedience consists in acting at the bidding of external authority, it would have no place in a state where the government is vested in the whole people, and where laws are made by common consent. (48) In such a society the people would remain free, whether the laws were added to or diminished, inasmuch as it would not be done on external authority, but their own free consent. (49) The reverse happens when the sovereign power is vested in one man, for all act at his bidding; and, therefore, unless they had been trained from the first to depend on the words of their ruler, the latter would find it difficult, in case of need, to abrogate liberties once conceded, and impose new laws.

(50) From these universal considerations, let us pass on to the kingdom of the Jews. (51) The Jews when they first came out of Egypt were not bound by any national laws, and were therefore free to ratify any laws they liked, or to make new ones, and were at liberty to set up a government and occupy a territory wherever they chose. (52) However, they, were entirely unfit to frame a wise code of laws and to keep the sovereign power vested in the community; they were all uncultivated and sunk in a wretched slavery, therefore the sovereignty was bound to remain vested in the hands of one man who would rule the rest and keep them under constraint, make laws and interpret them. (53) This sovereignty was easily retained by Moses, because he surpassed the rest in virtue and persuaded the people of the fact, proving it by many testimonies (see Exod. chap. xiv., last verse, and chap. xix:9). (54) He then, by the Divine virtue he possessed, made laws and ordained them for the people, taking the greatest care that they should be obeyed willingly and not through fear, being specially induced to adopt this course by the

obstinate nature of the Jews, who would not have submitted to be ruled solely by constraint; and also by the imminence of war, for it is always better to inspire soldiers with a thirst for glory than to terrify them with threats; each man will then strive to distinguish himself by valour and courage, instead of merely trying to escape punishment. (55) Moses, therefore, by his virtue and the Divine command, introduced a religion, so that the people might do their duty from devotion rather than fear. (56) Further, he bound them over by benefits, and prophesied many advantages in the future; nor were his laws very severe, as anyone may see for himself, especially if he remarks the number of circumstances necessary in order to procure the conviction of an accused person.

(57) Lastly, in order that the people which could not govern itself should be entirely dependent on its ruler, he left nothing to the free choice of individuals (who had hitherto been slaves); the people could do nothing but remember the law, and follow the ordinances laid down at the good pleasure of their ruler; they were not allowed to plough, to sow, to reap, nor even to eat; to clothe themselves, to shave, to rejoice, or in fact to do anything whatever as they liked, but were bound to follow the directions given in the law; and not only this, but they were obliged to have marks on their door-posts, on their hands, and between their eyes to admonish them to perpetual obedience.

(58) This, then, was the object of the ceremonial law, that men should do nothing of their own free will, but should always act under external authority, and should continually confess by their actions and thoughts that they were not their own masters, but were entirely under the control of others.

(59) From all these considerations it is clearer than day that ceremonies have nothing to do with a state of blessedness, and that those mentioned in the Old Testament, i.e. the whole Mosaic Law, had reference merely to the government of the Jews, and merely temporal advantages.

(60) As for the Christian rites, such as baptism, the Lord's Supper, festivals, public prayers, and any other observances which are, and always have been, common to all Christendom, if they were instituted by Christ or His Apostles (which is open to doubt), they were instituted as external signs of the universal church, and not as having anything to do with blessedness, or possessing any sanctity in themselves. (61) Therefore, though such ceremonies were not ordained for the sake of upholding a government, they were ordained for the preservation of a society, and accordingly he who lives alone is not bound by them: nay, those who live in a country where the Christian religion is forbidden, are bound to abstain from such rites, and can none the less live in a state of blessedness. (62) We have an example of this in Japan, where the Christian religion is forbidden, and the Dutch who live there are enjoined by their East India Company not to practise any outward rites of religion. (63) I need not cite other examples, though it would be easy to prove my point from the fundamental principles of the New Testament, and to adduce many confirmatory instances; but I pass on the more willingly, as I am anxious to proceed to my next proposition. (64) I will now, therefore, pass on to what I proposed to treat of in the second part of this chapter, namely, what persons are bound to believe in the narratives contained in Scripture, and how far they are so bound. (65) Examining this question

by the aid of natural reason, I will proceed as follows.

(66) If anyone wishes to persuade his fellows for or against anything which is not self-evident, he must deduce his contention from their admissions, and convince them either by experience or by ratiocination; either by appealing to facts of natural experience, or to self-evident intellectual axioms. (67) Now unless the experience be of such a kind as to be clearly and distinctly understood, though it may convince a man, it will not have the same effect on his mind and disperse the clouds of his doubt so completely as when the doctrine taught is deduced entirely from intellectual axioms - that is, by the mere power of the understanding and logical order, and this is especially the case in spiritual matters which have nothing to do with the senses.

(68) But the deduction of conclusions from general truths a priori, usually requires a long chain of arguments, and, moreover, very great caution, acuteness, and self-restraint - qualities which are not often met with; therefore people prefer to be taught by experience rather than deduce their conclusion from a few axioms, and set them out in logical order. (69) Whence it follows, that if anyone wishes to teach a doctrine to a whole nation (not to speak of the whole human race), and to be understood by all men in every particular, he will seek to support his teaching with experience, and will endeavour to suit his reasonings and the definitions of his doctrines as far as possible to the understanding of the common people, who form the majority of mankind, and he will not set them forth in logical sequence nor adduce the definitions which serve to establish them. (70) Otherwise he writes only for the learned - that is, he will be understood by only a small proportion of the human race.

(71) All Scripture was written primarily for an entire people, and secondarily for the whole human race; therefore its contents must necessarily be adapted as far as possible to the understanding of the masses, and proved only by examples drawn from experience. (72) We will explain ourselves more clearly. (73) The chief speculative doctrines taught in Scripture are the existence of God, or a Being Who made all things, and Who directs and sustains the world with consummate wisdom; furthermore, that God takes the greatest thought for men, or such of them as live piously and honourably, while He punishes, with various penalties, those who do evil, separating them from the good. (74) All this is proved in Scripture entirely through experience-that is, through the narratives there related. (75) No definitions of doctrine are given, but all the sayings and reasonings are adapted to the understanding of the masses. (76) Although experience can give no clear knowledge of these things, nor explain the nature of God, nor how He directs and sustains all things, it can nevertheless teach and enlighten men sufficiently to impress obedience and devotion on their minds.

(77) It is now, I think, sufficiently clear what persons are bound to believe in the Scripture narratives, and in what degree they are so bound, for it evidently follows from what has been said that the knowledge of and belief in them is particularly necessary to the masses whose intellect is not capable of perceiving things clearly and distinctly. (78) Further, he who denies them because he does not believe that God exists or takes thought for men and the world, may be accounted impious; but a man who is ignorant of them, and nevertheless knows by natural reason that God exists, as we have said, and has a true plan of life, is altogether blessed - yes, more

blessed than the common herd of believers, because besides true opinions he possesses also a true and distinct conception. (79) Lastly, he who is ignorant of the Scriptures and knows nothing by the light of reason, though he may not be impious or rebellious, is yet less than human and almost brutal, having none of God's gifts.

(80) We must here remark that when we say that the knowledge of the sacred narrative is particularly necessary to the masses, we do not mean the knowledge of absolutely all the narratives in the Bible, but only of the principal ones, those which, taken by themselves, plainly display the doctrine we have just stated, and have most effect over men's minds.

(81) If all the narratives in Scripture were necessary for the proof of this doctrine, and if no conclusion could be drawn without the general consideration of every one of the histories contained in the sacred writings, truly the conclusion and demonstration of such doctrine would overtask the understanding and strength not only of the masses, but of humanity; who is there who could give attention to all the narratives at once, and to all the circumstances, and all the scraps of doctrine to be elicited from such a host of diverse histories? (82) I cannot believe that the men who have left us the Bible as we have it were so abounding in talent that they attempted setting about such a method of demonstration, still less can I suppose that we cannot understand Scriptural doctrine till we have given heed to the quarrels of Isaac, the advice of Achitophel to Absalom, the civil war between Jews and Israelites, and other similar chronicles; nor can I think that it was more difficult to teach such doctrine by means of history to the Jews of early times, the contemporaries of Moses, than it was to the contemporaries of Esdras. (83) But more will be said on this point hereafter, we may now only note that the masses are only bound to know those histories which can most powerfully dispose their mind to obedience and devotion. (84) However, the masses are not sufficiently skilled to draw conclusions from what they read, they take more delight in the actual stories, and in the strange and unlooked-for issues of events than in the doctrines implied; therefore, besides reading these narratives, they are always in need of pastors or church ministers to explain them to their feeble intelligence.

(85) But not to wander from our point, let us conclude with what has been our principal object - namely, that the truth of narratives, be they what they may, has nothing to do with the Divine law, and serves for nothing except in respect of doctrine, the sole element which makes one history better than another. (86) The narratives in the Old and New Testaments surpass profane history, and differ among themselves in merit simply by reason of the salutary doctrines which they inculcate. (87) Therefore, if a man were to read the Scripture narratives believing the whole of them, but were to give no heed to the doctrines they contain, and make no amendment in his life, he might employ himself just as profitably in reading the Koran or the poetic drama, or ordinary chronicles, with the attention usually given to such writings; on the other hand, if a man is absolutely ignorant of the Scriptures, and none the less has right opinions and a true plan of life, he is absolutely blessed and truly possesses in himself the spirit of Christ.

(88) The Jews are of a directly contrary way of thinking, for they hold that true opinions and a true plan of life are of no service in attaining blessedness, if their possessors have arrived at them by the light of reason only, and not like the documents prophetically revealed to Moses. (89)

Maimonides ventures openly to make this assertion: "Every man who takes to heart the seven precepts and diligently follows them, is counted with the pious among the nation, and an heir of the world to come; that is to say, if he takes to heart and follows them because God ordained them in the law, and revealed them to us by Moses, because they were of aforetime precepts to the sons of Noah: but he who follows them as led thereto by reason, is not counted as a dweller among the pious or among the wise of the nations." (90) Such are the words Of Maimonides, to which R. Joseph, the son of Shem Job, adds in his book which he calls "Kebod Elohim, or God's Glory," that although Aristotle (whom he considers to have written the best ethics and to be above everyone else) has not omitted anything that concerns true ethics, and which he has adopted in his own book, carefully following the lines laid down, yet this was not able to suffice for his salvation, inasmuch as he embraced his doctrines in accordance with the dictates of reason and not as Divine documents prophetically revealed.

(91) However, that these are mere figments, and are not supported by Scriptural authority will, I think, be sufficiently evident to the attentive reader, so that an examination of the theory will be sufficient for its refutation. (92) It is not my purpose here to refute the assertions of those who assert that the natural light of reason can teach nothing, of any value concerning the true way of salvation. (93) People who lay no claims to reason for themselves, are not able to prove by reason this their assertion; and if they hawk about something superior to reason, it is a mere figment, and far below reason, as their general method of life sufficiently shows. (94) But there is no need to dwell upon such persons. (95) I will merely add that we can only judge of a man by his works. (96) If a man abounds in the fruits of the Spirit, charity, joy, peace, long-suffering, kindness, goodness, faith, gentleness, chastity, against which, as Paul says (Gal. v:22), there is no law, such an one, whether he be taught by reason only or by the Scripture only, has been in very truth taught by God, and is altogether blessed. (97) Thus have I said all that I undertook to say concerning Divine law.

End of Part 1

Made in the USA
Las Vegas, NV
21 October 2021